WOODLAND ECOLOGY

WOODLAND ECOLOGY

By

G.

ERNEST NEAL

SECOND EDITION

HARVARD UNIVERSITY PRESS
CAMBRIDGE, MASSACHUSETTS

CONTENTS

LIST OF PLATES

LINE ILLUSTRATIONS

PREFACE

WOODLAND is one of the most complex communities of animals and plants, and it would be a bold man who tried to write a comprehensive book on its ecology. This introduction to the subject is not intended to be a summary of existing knowledge ; anyone who has practical experience of the problems involved is only too well aware how little he knows and how little is known of the intricate inter-relationships of the numerous woodland organisms.

This book is written primarily for sixth form, and first year university students, but it is hoped that it may also be of some use to that increasing body of naturalists who are not content with mere records, but who wish to discover more about the lives and relationships of the animals and plants they discover.

The book is written from the practical standpoint of the student who wishes to find out for himself the general pattern of woodland composition. It is based largely on a study of one woodland community over a period of about four years carried out by the author, working in conjunction with sixth-form biology students at Taunton School, and at times on his own.

The amount of ecology that can be done during the two or three years of a sixth-form course varies considerably from school to school. Some schools are fortunate in being situated in ideal country, and where much out-of-school work can be attempted ; others are faced with transport problems and lack of time ; and the majority have to cope with the difficulties of a rigid time-table and the conflicting interests of a full school life. In spite of difficulties, however, I am convinced that even with very limited time the attempt is very well worth while. The whole biology course springs to life when a project of this kind is attempted, and the students become aware of the wider aspects of the subject.

It is very easy when studying such a complex community as woodland to be overwhelmed by the number of organisms living there, and literally to miss the wood for the trees in consequence. In fact it has been suggested that because of its complexity woodland should not be studied as an ecological habitat until much experience has been gained. I feel, however, that for schools this view is unjustified as it is a community which has a considerable appeal, and although a complete survey is seldom possible, enough can be done quite quickly to illustrate the main principles upon which ecology is based.

For this work to be successful it is advisable to have a background picture of the wood as a whole unit. This acts as a broadsheet for all detailed work carried out. It is neither necessary nor as a rule advisable to try to cover all aspects, but by concentrating on microhabitats within the wood, or on a single species or factor, a lot can be achieved, and the results can then be related to the over-all picture.

It is hoped that this main concept of wholeness will become more apparent as the book proceeds and that the emphasis on principle as illustrated by detailed examples will help to broaden the concept.

It is not possible to deal adequately with the many aspects of woodland ecology in a book of this kind. Under-emphasis will be apparent on some points, over-emphasis on others, and important studies may be omitted altogether. We have tried to emphasize those parts of the subject which are within the powers of the average student with limited time available for the study.

It would be convenient if this book could be arranged in a logical sequence starting with the geology and proceeding through soil studies to the flora and ultimately to the fauna. The practical study of an area, however, cannot be carried out in this way. Observations have to be made at different times and seasons, and knowledge is gradually built up from a rather heterogeneous mass of details. Although the ideal of a logical sequence has been kept in mind, it has been modified in places to conform to the methods of practical enquiry.

The study of woodland is in its infancy. There is so much to discover, so many problems to tackle, so much scope for initiative, that by the time you have spent a few days—and nights—observing and recording, your interest will probably have blossomed into something much deeper and you will find it hard to give it up.

The most essential attribute of the ecologist is the possession of the right attitude of mind. He must combine the great enthusiasm and powers of accurate observation of the old naturalists with the ability to synthesize the details into a living whole. He must be asking himself all the time why this organism should be here. What part does it play in the life of the community ? What are its relationships with other types ? How is it adapted to the complex factors of its environment ? And, having thought out some of the answers, he must put them to the test by any means he can devise to see if he is right or wrong.

I have followed the principle of using English names where these are familiar, adding the scientific name for the first few times of mentioning. For the plants I have followed the names found in *The Flora of the British Isles*, by Clapham, A. R., Tutin, T. G., and Warburg, E. F. (1952). For the insects I have relied on *A Check List of British Insects*, by Kloet, G. S., and Hincks, W. D. (1945).

It is impossible to write any book on ecology without being indebted to a host of others whose labours have resulted in so many indispensable facts and ideas. Of these I cannot over-estimate the pioneering work of Dr. Charles Elton and Professor Tansley who have done so much through their writings to put animal and plant ecology on a sound basis in this country.

I am also very grateful to Alan Dale for helpful advice and criticisms, and to L. C. Comber, W. H. Dowdeswell, John Sankey and R. B. Whellock for reading through the manuscript and making valuable suggestions. I should also like to thank the various members of my sixth-forms who have co-operated with me in this study of woodland. Of the latter I would specially mention John Ryland who carried out a lot of excellent work on the flora of Thurlbear.

I would also like to thank the Commissioners of Crown Lands for giving us permission to work in Thurlbear woods.

ERNEST G. NEAL.

PREFACE TO SECOND EDITION

This edition has been enlarged by adding a chapter on succession. This illustrates how the main changes which occur when grassland reverts to woodland may to some extent be deduced from a study of the present flora.

One of the biggest problems of any ecological study is the identification of the flora and the fauna. It was therefore decided to extend the bibliography by adding a selection of the more useful books available for this purpose.

It is also hoped that the additional illustrations will increase the usefulness of the book.

January, 1958.   ERNEST G. NEAL.

CHAPTER I

GENERAL CONSIDERATIONS

BEFORE starting on our detailed investigation of one woodland community, it is useful to summarize the general characteristics of the more important types of woodland found in Britain, so that the smaller study can fit into the wider picture. Only floral composition will be taken into account as reference to animal types in such a brief summary would only distract from the main principles.

Woodland is the natural climax vegetation of much of the British Isles. Except for the northern part of Scotland and areas of high altitude, the vegetation, if left alone by man, would quickly revert to deciduous woodland once more.

As the last ice belt retreated some ten thousand years ago, the British Isles—then a peninsula of Europe—was colonized by woodland consisting mainly of pine and birch. Later, as the climate became warmer and the rainfall increased, oak became the dominant tree, with alder in the wetter parts. The natural pine and birch forests still remain in parts of northern Scotland, but there is little left of truly natural oak woodland in England today. Much of these natural woods was felled by the early residents of Britain so that crops could be grown and grazing animals kept. Later, the timber was used for construction and many commercial purposes. It was not until about four hundred years ago that planting of woodland to compensate for the felling started on a small scale.

Although most of the woodland of today is semi-natural, it does not necessarily differ very much from the natural woods of the past. Our woods are still dominated by oak, beech, ash, alder, birch or pine, as they were several thousand years ago, and although some differ from natural woods by having trees mainly of the same age, due to planting, others show natural regeneration.

The dominant type of tree in Britain is determined by a

number of factors, of which soil condition is the most important. The type of soil tips the balance between oak and beech. On heavy clays oak is more vigorous and tends to oust the beech, while on chalk and limestones the converse is usually true. This has given rise to the suggestion that beech is a calcicole, but this is not so as it will grow strongly on other soils if oak competition is removed.

A calcareous soil favours the formation of ash woods. These colonize quickly as they fruit freely and germinate very easily, but after some time they are usually superseded in the south by the more vigorous beech. The latter do not form an adequate number of seedlings for colonization every year, but eventually, with their taller growth and shadowing effect, they top the ashes and prevent adequate photosynthesis from taking place and the ash trees die.

When the soil becomes very damp, alder may take the place of oak as a dominant, but there are few large areas of alderwood today. Typically, it is found on the edges of marshes, of rivers, and more extensively in the fen district.

Birch woods are often found in the south on sandy soils where oak woods have been felled. If oaks are allowed to develop, they tend to supersede the birch, just as beech does the ash. In the north birches can stand a slightly higher altitude than oak. Pine is often associated with birch on sandy soil in southern England, and also in the Scottish Highlands.

The dominant tree largely determines the type of flora in a wood and hence, directly or indirectly, the fauna. This is due largely to the amount of shade cast and the duration of that shade phase.

Of the four most distinctive types, ashwood, oakwood, beechwood and pinewood, the ash, with its compound leaves, casts least shade. It also comes into full leaf later in the spring than other deciduous types, and leaf fall is often earlier. Thus more light is able to penetrate during the shade phase and there is a longer season of growth for other plants in the wood. In consequence, a shrub layer is usually conspicuous in an ash wood, with hazel (*Corylus avellana*) and hawthorn (*Cratægus monogyna*) as prominent members. A number of lime-loving shrubs may also be present when the soil is calcareous such as dogwood (*Cornus sanguinea*), wayfaring tree (*Viburnum lantana*), spindle (*Euonymus europaeus*) and privet (*Ligustrum vulgare*).

This shrub layer in turn casts its shade and influences the growth of the field layer. This shade does not become dense until well into May in the south, so that the early-flowering herbaceous perennials can flourish in the early spring. Thus three layers or strata of vegetation can be distinguished in an ash wood—tree, shrub, and field layer. A fourth layer may also be found, consisting mainly of mosses under the field layer, but this is not always a conspicuous feature.

There are two species of oak which dominate our woodland, the pendunculate oak (*Quercus robur*) with its acorns on long stalks, and the durmast oak (*Quercus sessiliflora*) with its acorns almost without stalks. The former is characteristic of southern and eastern England, while the latter is most common in the south-west, west and north. Both kinds, however, have been planted commonly and there is much overlap, both species and their hybrids often growing together in the same wood.

Oak casts rather more shade than ash, but a lot of light still comes through, especially when the oaks are in open canopy— that is when the ultimate branches of neighbouring trees do

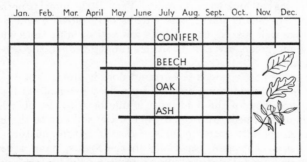

FIG. 1. The duration of the shade phase in woods dominated by Ash Oak, Beech and Conifer.

not touch. The shade phase is rather longer than in an ash-wood, but there is still time for a varied field layer to flourish in the spring. As in an ashwood, the shrub layer and field layer are usually well developed, but they differ widely according to soil conditions.

On medium clays and loams which are not too wet, hazel is usually the dominant shrub, and the field layer is very varied and prolific. On heavier clay which is often waterlogged in winter, alders (*Alnus glutinosa*) are often found with the oaks, and sallows (*Salix spp.*) are present in the shrub layer. In the field layer pendulous sedge (*Carex pendula*) is often conspicuous.

Oakwoods on drier, more shallow and slightly acid soils have less shrubs and the field layer is often dominated by bracken (*Pteridium aquilinum*), while bluebells (*Endymion non-scriptus*), wood soft grass (*Holcus mollis*), wood sage (*Teucrium scorodonia*) and foxgloves (*Digitalis purpurea*) are conspicuous in the field layer.

Finally, on very acid sandy soils, birch (*Betula sp.*) is usually associated with the oaks, which are often poorly developed. Shrubs are few, and the field layer may consist of such plants as heather (*Calluna vulgaris*), whortleberry (*Vaccinium myrtillus*), tormentil (*Potentilla erecta*) and heath bedstraw (*Galium saxatile*).

In beech woods the shade is considerable, due to the shape of the leaves and their mosaic. Very little light penetrates during the shade phase, and shrubs only develop where the trees are well spaced, except for a few yew or holly trees which, being evergreen, are able to utilize the light when the beeches are leafless.

In some beech woods the ground flora is almost absent, the floor of the wood being covered by a deep litter of old leaves. The sparseness of the field layer is due both to the poor light for photosynthesis, and the drying of the soil due to the mass of beech rootlets near the surface absorbing the moisture.

Other beechwoods, especially in the loams, have a better developed field layer including bramble (*Rubus fructicosus*), wood sorrel (*Oxalis acetosella*), ivy (*Hedera helix*), dog's

PLATE I

A. Thurlbear Wood from the west (November), showing the oaks in closed canopy with hazel in the shrub layer.

B. Caterpillar of the Alder Moth. In the early stages it resembles a bird-dropping.

PLATE II

A. Primrose leaves showing leaf mines formed by the larvae of small moths.

B. Oak log attacked by fungi. As the bark becomes loosened in the process shelter is provided for woodlice and insects.

mercury (*Mercurialis perennis*), hairy violet (*Viola hirta*) and many others, but it is never so prolific as that found in oak or ash woods, and most species are those which are capable of making good use of the early spring light phase. The shade phase lasts longer in beech woods than in ash or oak woods.

Pines, being evergreen, cast a deep shade all the year round, and if the trees are close together no shrub or field layer will be present except towards the edges of the wood where lateral light can penetrate.

In natural pine woods the trees are often further apart and a heathy field layer develops which includes heather (*Calluna vulgaris*) and whortleberry (*Vaccinium myrtillus*).

CHAPTER II

THE AREA OF WOODLAND CHOSEN FOR DETAILED INVESTIGATION

As woods differ so much in detailed structure, according to local factors, it is useful to describe one area as a fairly typical example of a woodland community, and we have chosen for this purpose an area known as Thurlbear Woods, some five miles to the south of Taunton in the county of Somerset.

The main region of about 32 acres is dominated by oaks in open canopy with coppiced hazel in the shrub layer. The oaks were planted at different times in various parts of the wood, and at the time of writing a number have already been felled for timber, their age being approximately one hundred and twenty years. Thus small areas are present with no tree layer at all.

The altitude varies from two hundred to two hundred and eighty feet, most of the area being fairly flat but with a steep slope on the western edge.

The wood is situated on the Lower Lias and represents an interesting outcrop of calcareous country in an otherwise rather non-calcareous district. This limestone has an important effect on the flora of the wood.

Preliminary Survey

The object of the study was to build up an integrated picture of the whole community, and as the plant life provides the scaffolding of the wood on which the more mobile animal population can be built, the first thing to do was to concentrate on the botanical side.

Preliminary observations were made of the whole area, and it was at once obvious that, although the general pattern of structure was similar, there were important variations in the flora in certain parts.

6

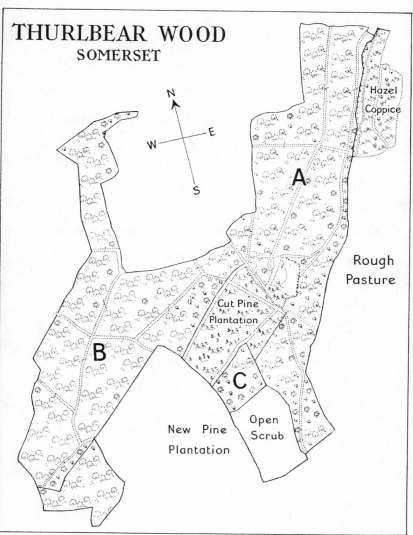

THURLBEAR WOOD
SOMERSET

N
W E
S

Hazel Coppice

A

Rough Pasture

B

Cut Pine Plantation

C

Open Scrub

New Pine Plantation

FIG. 2.   Thurlbear Wood.   *Crown Copyright.*

A 25-inch to the mile Ordnance Survey map was used and a number of rough copies of the area were duplicated. The main areas of variation were then mapped out.

The variation was most obvious in the spring when the dominant plants of the field layer could easily be seen. Three main regions were noted, and for convenience called A, B and C.

B was dominated by oaks (*Quercus robur*) in open canopy, with hazel (*Corylus avellana*) the main species in the shrub layer. In the field layer, wood anemones (*Anemone nemorosa*) were dominant in the prevernal aspect, but bluebells (*Endymion non-scriptus*) took their place a little later. Ivy (*Hedera helix*) was present all over the area, and in the denser parts became dominant. Dog's mercury (*Mercurialis perennis*) was rare. This region covered the southern half of the wood and sloped steeply on its southern and western edges.

A was flatter, and although the tree and shrub layers were similar to B, anemones were rare and ivy was mainly dominant. Bluebells were present in the lighter areas, but were never dominant. Dog's mercury was not present in any quantity. This region formed the northern part of the wood.

C was a small area bordering the very calcareous pasture on the east. Again oaks and hazels were dominant in their respective layers, but there were no anemones, and bluebells and dog's mercury were co-dominant in the field layer, forming a thick carpet.

Two other small adjoining areas were of interest, D and E. Here there were no oaks and the hazels had been coppiced. In D the hazels had been coppiced in 1945, and in E in 1949. This gave us an opportunity of studying the effect of coppicing on the field layer.

Lastly it was obvious that local areas in the wood were very wet all the year, with standing water and sticky yellow mud much in evidence. These areas had their own characteristic flora. Sallows (*Salix spp.*) were present in the shrub layer and the pendulous sedge (*Carex pendula*) often dominated the field layer.

This preliminary survey of the area provided a basis for more detailed study of each region. This was carried out in order to discover exactly how each region differed in composition, after which the reasons for the differences could be investigated.

CHAPTER III

FLORAL COMPOSITION

Method of Detailed Study

WHEN studying the details of the flora of each area, we were at once faced with the difficulty of correlating a vast number of random observations, so a scheme was drawn up whereby attention could be focused on the more important aspects.

The first thing was to identify all the plants in tree, shrub and herb layers in each region. This could not be done at one season only, but as further species came into flower these were added to the list.

A large chart was then made, on which all the important plants were listed, and appropriate columns left for certain details in respect of each plant which could be added from time to time throughout the year. The facts which we wished to discover included the relative frequency in the main areas A, B, and C, the period of photosynthesis for each species, the period of flowering, the life form of the plant, whether underground storage organs were present, and if so what type, the depth of the rooting system, the methods of pollination and the agents concerned, the means of propagation including ways by which seeds and fruits were dispersed and any other adaptation to woodland conditions, especially those concerned with light. In this way we hoped to build up a fairly complete picture of the part played by the various plants in the community throughout the year and the inter-relation of some of them.

This method of gradually building up a picture from a mass of somewhat random observations had several great advantages. It helped to emphasize the more significant similarities and differences between the species, and it showed up the gaps in our knowledge. During the second year of work it was possible to concentrate on the significant points, experimenting and observing to confirm or reject the previous year's findings, also to concentrate on the omissions which, on a chart, appear so obvious.

(1) *Frequency*

The dominant plants in the tree and shrub layers were invariably oak and hazel respectively in all parts of the main wood. This was a help when comparing the members of the field layer as it reduced the number of variable factors by two. The dominant plants in the field layer were sometimes quite obvious by observation only, but when there was any doubt counts were made of the number of the plants in question in a number of small quadrats taken at random in the particular area.

It should perhaps be emphasized here that although the term dominant is often an indication of frequency it is a broader concept than that of frequency alone. A dominant plant exerts the greatest influence on other members of the community, and if it was not present the whole appearance of that community would alter. Thus a few large oak trees may have a far greater effect on the rest of the wood than a larger number of young ash trees growing with them.

Reliable figures of frequency given in percentages are only useful when large numbers of samples are counted, and the great labour involved in counting each species in a large number of quadrats did not appear to be justified. A rough idea of frequency was obtained quite easily, however, by observation alone, and although not strictly accurate, the method was sufficiently useful to bring out any considerable variation in different areas. The usual categories of abundant, frequent, occasional or rare were used, the term local being used in addition when appropriate. For this work several observers patrolled the area keeping certain plants in mind, and their opinions of frequency were compared. The same observers were used in each case for the various types, so that error due to the personal factor was reduced.

One difficulty with this observational method is the seasonal

TABLE I

FREQUENCIES

ENGLISH NAME	LATIN NAME	AREA A	AREA B	AREA C
Oak . . .	*Quercus robur* .	D	D	D
Ash . . .	*Fraxinus excelsior* .	F	F	R
Hornbeam . .	*Carpinus betulus* .	R	—	—
Hazel . . .	*Corylus avellana* .	D	D	D
Sallow . .	*Salix caprea* .	O	O	—
Hawthorn . .	*Crataegus monogyna* .	O	O	O
Maple . . .	*Acer campestre* .	F	O	A
Privet . . .	*Ligustrum vulgare* .	F	F	F
Holly . . .	*Ilex aquifolium* .	O	R	—
Spindle . .	*Euonymus europaeus* .	O	O	O
Dogwood . .	*Cornus sanguinea* .	F	F	F
Wayfaring tree .	*Viburnum lantana* .	O	O	R
Guelder rose .	*Viburnum opulus* .	O	O	—
Dog rose . .	*Rosa canina* .	O	O	R
Blackberry . .	*Rubus fructicosus* .	LF	LF	O
Honeysuckle .	*Lonicera periclymenum* .	F	LA	O
Ivy . . .	*Hedera helix* .	D	LD	LF
Black Bryony .	*Tamus communis* .	LF	LF	O
Pendulous sedge .	*Carex pendula* .	LD	LF	—
Burdock . .	*Arctium vulgare* .	O	O	O
Fœtid Iris . .	*Iris foetidissima*.	F	F	O
Wood Anemone .	*Anemone nemorosa* .	O	D	—
Bluebell . .	*Endymion non-scriptus* .	A	A	Co-D
Dog's Mercury .	*Mercurialis perennis* .	O	R	Co-D
Yellow Archangel .	*Galeobdolon luteum* .	LF	LF	O
Lesser Celandine .	*Ranunculus ficaria* .	F	LF	F
Primrose . .	*Primula vulgaris* .	F	A	LF
Cuckoo Pint .	*Arum maculatum* .	O	F	LF
Goldilocks . .	*Ranunculus auricomus* .	O	O	O
Violet . . .	*Viola hirta* .	F	F	F
Bugle . . .	*Ajuga reptans* .	O	LF	LF
Wood Spurge .	*Euphorbia amygdaloides* .	LF	F	F
Woodruff . .	*Asperula odorata* .	LA	LA	LF
Earthnut . .	*Conopodium major* .	F	O	—
Enchanter's Nightshade	*Circaea lutetiana* .	F	F	F
Early Purple Orchid	*Orchis mascula* . .	F	F	F
Spotted Orchid .	*Orchis fuchsii* . .	O	O	O
Butterfly Orchid .	*Platanthera chlorantha*.	R	R	O
Twayblade Orchid .	*Listera ovata* . .	O	O	F
Bird's Nest Orchid .	*Neottia nidus-avis* .	O	O	—

KEY

D	= Dominant.	O = Occasional.
Co-D	= Co-Dominant.	R = Rare.
A	= Abundant.	L = Prefix meaning " locally ".
F	= Frequent.	

factor. Some plants are very obvious at some seasons and much less so at others, and we found it useful to re-check frequency on different visits.

The plants which appeared to have the most significant differences in frequency in the various parts were wood anemone, dog's mercury and ivy, all of which were dominant or abundant in one part of the wood while absent or much reduced in other parts.

Having obtained a fair knowledge of the main types of plants in the various strata, and a rough indication of their frequency, it was possible to compare the species with those found in other well-defined habitats. It soon became obvious that the majority of the species were true woodland types. If they occurred elsewhere, it was in habitats which shared some of the environmental factors of a wood. For example, dog's mercury is occasionally met with in dense hedgerows where light is scarce as in woods. Bluebells are not unusually found associated with bracken, where again a dense shade is cast. Climbers such as honeysuckle and black bryony are often found in hedges and obtain their light in the same manner as in woods, by climbing.

Other species were found only along the paths or at the edges of the wood. Single specimens of plants which were extremely common outside the wood were seen, indicating a type out of its natural habitat. These plants we noted, but did not seriously consider as they provided the exceptions. It was only by concentrating on the true woodland types that we could hope for an understanding of inter-relationships.

The urgent and most fundamental question was : Why were these typical plants found in woods and seldom elsewhere? Was it that they were specially adapted structurally and physiologically to the physical and biotic factors typical of a wood while the plants which lived in other habitats were not? Could they compete better with other species under woodland conditions than elsewhere? To answer these questions it was necessary to study all the typical plants as extensively as possible to see if any structural or physiological characteristics were common to a lot of them, and if so, whether these factors helped them to live in that particular environment.

(2) *Period of Photosynthesis throughout the Year*

Under the difficult light conditions of a wood, it was thought that the period during which the plants of the field layer could photosynthesize was important. It was necessary to assume that if the plant had adequate chlorophyll and the temperature was not abnormally low, photosynthesis would be taking place at that season to some extent. This assumption was found to be justified by testing for starch or sugar in the first green leaves of emerging plants in early spring, with positive results except in extreme conditions of cold. In other words, it appeared that when seasonal conditions were suitable for growth in a particular species so that new leaves were formed, photosynthesis could also take place. Further investigation along these lines for all species in a wood, including evergreen and winter-green types, would be useful and probably lead to interesting results. It was also noted when the leaves turned yellow or died down later in the season.

When the period of photosynthesis was plotted for each species, it was at once apparent that there were four main patterns. First, there were the short-phase plants which usually opened their leaves very early in the year, but did not persist for long after the tree and shrub layer had come into full leaf ; these have been described as pre-vernal types. They included bluebell (*Endymion non-scriptus*), lesser celandine (*Ranunculus ficaria*), cuckoo pint (*Arum maculatum*), wood anemone (*Anemone nemorosa*), goldilocks (*Ranunculus auricomus*) and some of the orchids.

Secondly, there were those which persisted during the shade phase and continued to photosynthesize sufficiently for active, though usually slower, growth during that period. Those have been described as summer-green types and included dog's mercury (*Mercurialis perennis*), honeysuckle (*Lonicera periclymenum*), black bryony (*Tamus communis*), enchanter's nightshade (*Circœa lutetiana*) and wood burdock (*Arctium vulgare*).

The third class included species which formed new leaves in the autumn which persisted through the winter, but these leaves were not nearly so numerous or well-developed as the

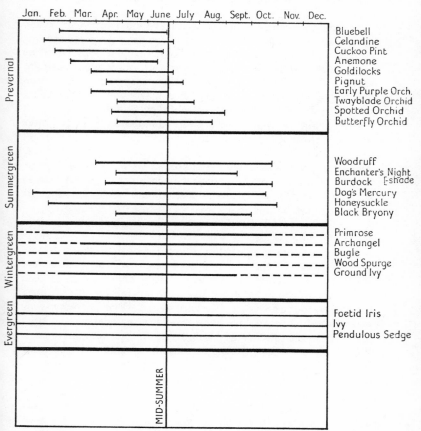

FIG. 3.   The Leaf Condition of Woodland Plants.

summer leaves. This group of winter-greens included arch-angel (*Galeobdolon luteum*), bugle (*Ajuga reptans*) and wood sanicle (*Sanicula europaea*).

Finally, there were those which were true evergreens, having normal foliage all the year. These included ivy (*Hedera helix*), foetid iris (*Iris foetidissima*) and pendulous sedge (*Carex pendula*).

It was sometimes difficult to determine exactly to what class a species belonged. Primroses, for example, appeared to come in the class of winter-greens as many plants persisted as tight rosettes of leaves during the winter, but during the shade phase individual plants behaved differently according to the density of the shade. In very dark parts the leaves turned yellow in June and died down, not being replaced until the autumn, but in lighter situations the leaves enlarged and persisted throughout the shade phase.

It was evident that the largest class was the pre-vernals. This group not only included the greatest number of typical woodland species, but also types which numerically were large, such as bluebells, celandine and anemone. However, not all the abundant or dominant species were in this category, as ivy was a very successful evergreen and dog's mercury a very successful summer-green.

It appeared, therefore, that adaptation to the shade condi-tion followed several lines in the plants of the field layer. First, those which by some means were able to take fullest advantage of the light phase, in spring storing up enough food for the rest of the year. Second, those which were physio-logically adapted to low light intensity so that they could photosynthesize sufficiently well for limited growth during the shade phase. Third, those summer-greens which were structurally adapted as climbers to get to the light. Fourth, those which could persist through the winter with reduced foliage, thus prolonging the period of photosynthesis to the maximum during the light phase. Lastly, those evergreens which, by having leaves all the year round, made the greatest use of all light available.

(3) *The Life Form*

Observations which helped to throw some light on the adaptations to woodland conditions were made on the life form of the plants. A modification of Raunkiaer's classification according to the position of perennating buds was used as follows :—

Phanerophytes where the winter buds were carried well up into the air, as on trees and the majority of shrubs.

Chamæphytes where the buds were situated close to the ground, but nevertheless freely exposed to the air.

Hemicryptophytes where the buds were hidden in the top-soil and protected by leaf litter, etc., but not hidden deep in the soil.

Geophytes where the buds were well below the surface of the soil.

Therophytes where the plants, being annuals, had their dormant bud inside the seed, the parent plant being dead.

Taking the British flora as a whole, one can say that it is mainly a hemicryptophytic one, but in the field layer of woodland this was found to be very far from the case, the highest proportion being of geophytes, hemicryptophytes and chamæphytes being present as well. Moreover, the geophytes contained some of the most characteristic and abundant woodland species such as bluebell, wood anemone, dog's mercury, lesser celandine, cuckoo pint and the orchids.

This preponderance of geophytes appears to be very significant as the perennating buds were associated with large stores of food in the rhizomes, corms, bulbs and tubers.

Another most significant fact about the woodland flora was the almost total absence of therophytes. If, however, we take the two points in conjunction, the presence of underground storage organs in the most typical plants, and the absence of annuals, it suggests that the geophytes with their abundant supply of stored food are able to produce vegetative structures very early in the year, thus enabling them to make the best use of the light phase. Annuals, however, would have less chance.

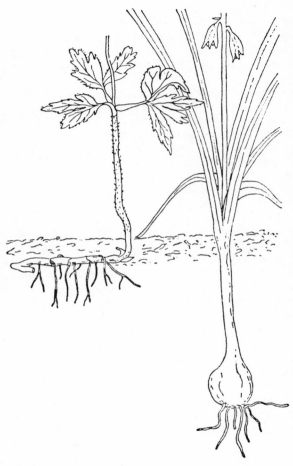

FIG. 4.   Rooting Systems of Wood Anemone and Bluebell showing how
different soil layers are utilized.

In the case of the therophytes, another factor comes in which would appear to be more important, that is the difficulty of competing as young seedlings with the already well-established and prolific perennial flora.

Specimens of each typical member of the field layer were carefully dug up in the spring and examined to see what kinds of food storage organs were present and at what depth they were to be found. Owing to the thickness of the clay it was not easy to separate out entire root systems in most cases, but it was usually possible to see what part of the soil was being tapped for water and salts.

The top two or three inches were tapped mainly by dog's mercury, wood anemones, ivy and hairy violet (*Viola hirta*), while below this level, bluebells, cuckoo pint (*Arum maculatum*), wood spurge (*Euphorbia amygdaloides*), and the orchids—early purple (*Orchis mascula*), butterfly (*Platanthera chlorantha*) and twayblade (*Listera ovata*) were present. It appeared from these observations that members of these two groups would not compete very much with each other, and this might be a factor which had a bearing on the distribution of dominants in the wood. We will leave discussion of this point until later when some of the other factors have been taken into account.

(4) *Period of Flowering*

Observations were made on the period of flowering of species in all strata in the wood, at the same time as the period of photosynthesis was being studied. When compiling dates of flowering, it was thought advisable to concentrate on the typical period of flowering for the species, ignoring the exceptional and odd specimens of common plants found flowering out of season.

Ideally the flowering range should be compiled from data collected over many years, but as a short term policy useful results can be obtained if all the dates apply to a single year, thus if it happens to be an early or late year the dates are more or less relative. This policy was adopted as relative dates were more important than actual dates for bringing out general principles.

It is customary to divide up the year into five seasons from the point of view of the flora—pre-vernal, vernal, æstival, autumnal and hiemal. These vary somewhat from year to year according to the weather in the earlier months, and in relation to locality. In the Taunton area of Somerset the spring is often early ; this was the case in 1950 when this table was compiled.

The pre-vernal aspect in this year was characteristic of the period from mid-February to mid-April. In the field layer dog's mercury was the first to bloom in any numbers, a few plants being found in flower as early as mid-January. A little later, primroses (*Primula vulgaris*) and violets (*Viola riviniana*) became prominent and by mid-March anemones and celandines (*Ranunculus ficaria*) had made their appearance. The full beauty of the pre-vernal aspect with its mass of flower was seen during the first fortnight of April. In the shrub layer the hazel flowered earliest, in fact, before the pre-vernal season was properly established (mid-January to early-March). Sallows blossomed towards the end of March.

The vernal aspect (mid-April until nearly the end of May) saw the flowering of the oaks in the tree layer. In the field layer bluebells took the place of the anemones, dog's mercury and primroses, while early purple orchids and bugle became more prominent. Violets continued to bloom, and goldilocks (*Ranunculus auricomus*), archangel (*Galeobdolon luteum*) and woodruff (*Asperula odorata*) became conspicuous. Cuckoo pint bloomed at the edges though seldom in the darker parts of the wood.

The æstival aspect (end of May until end of August), showed a marked reduction in the number of species blooming, though new ones made their appearance. Of these the most important were the four orchids—twayblade (*Listera ovata*), spotted (*Orchis fuchsii*), greater butterfly (*Platanthera chlorantha*) and birds' nest (*Neottia nidus-avis*) ; these bloomed in June. Enchanter's nightshade (*Circæa lutetiana*) followed

PLATE III

A. Butterfly and Spotted Orchids—flowers of the æstival aspect.

B. Wood Anemone—a typical co-dominant with bluebell in the field layer.

PLATE IV

A. Pre-vernal Herb Layer Flora, showing utilization of all available space.

B. Many woodland fungi act as saprophytes.

C. Sallow blossoms early in the year, and provides nectar for many species of insects.

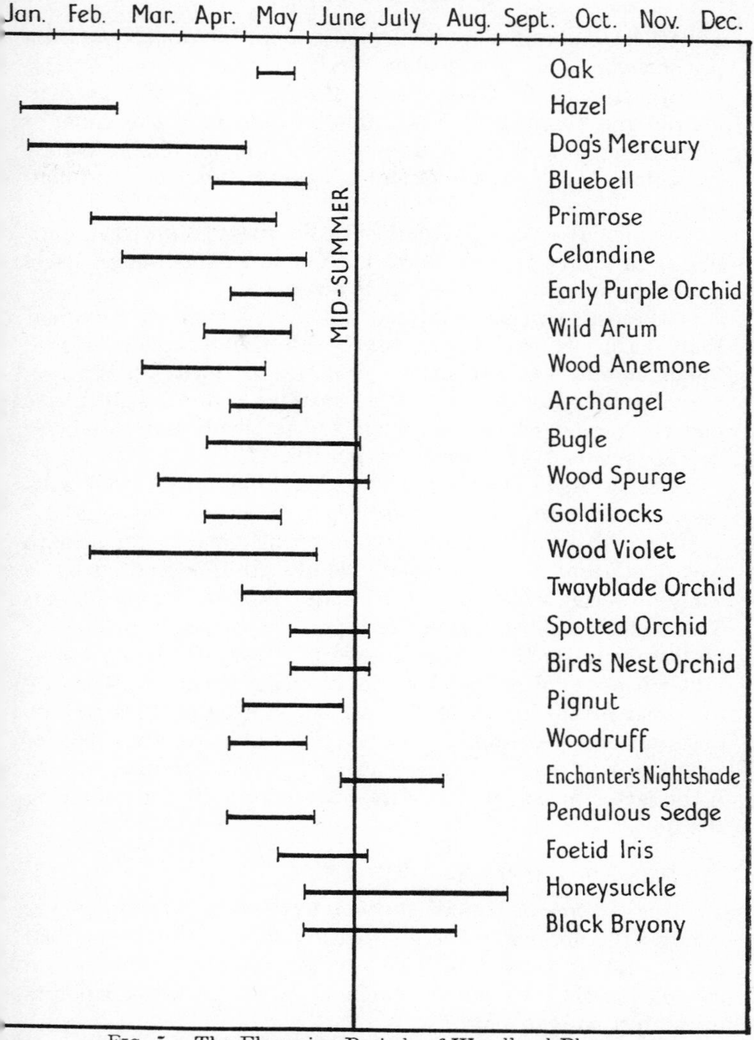

FIG. 5. The Flowering Periods of Woodland Plants.

a little later along with perforate St. John's wort (*Hypericum perforatum*) and the willow herb (*Epilobium montanum*) towards the edge of the rides. Black bryony (*Tamus communis*) and honeysuckle also came into bloom at this time.

No new flowers were seen during the autumnal aspect (September to November), though many fungi became conspicuous.

The hiemal aspect (December to February) showed no new plants in flower though towards the end of this season hazel and dog's mercury were again in bloom.

If these results are analysed it becomes strikingly evident that with few exceptions, nearly all the woodland plants bloom in the first half of the year, the majority in the pre-vernal and vernal aspects. This coincides with the light phase and the period when the foliage of the shrub and tree layer has not reached the maximum density.

This contrasts strongly with other habitats such as salt-marsh and heath, which are largely æstival and autumnal.

It would appear that early flowering was a response to woodland conditions, especially light. If this is so, why is early flowering necessary to the majority of woodland plants? The fact that flowering is the reproductive phase in the life history suggests that good light is necessary for this process, either because of pollination, the ripening of the seeds, or the dispersal of the seeds or fruits. To elucidate these points, observations were made whenever possible on the type of pollination of each plant—whether by wind or insects, and if the latter, what species of insect was actually seen entering the flower.

(5) *Pollination Methods*

Observations on many flowers were very incomplete as regards the species of insects visiting them and a great deal more work is needed on this aspect of the question before reliable conclusions can be reached. However, certain points of interest emerged.

Wind pollination was the usual method for the tree layer

where the oaks in early May produced an enormous quantity of pollen. The occasional ash and wych elm trees in this layer were also wind pollinated though hive bees have been known to visit the latter for pollen. Hazel, which was dominant in the shrub layer was also wind pollinated, though many of the other shrubs which occurred were pollinated by insects. These included sallow, hawthorn, maple, privet, holly, spindle, dogwood, wayfaring tree and guelder rose. The insect pollinated types, however, were numerically few and their position in the wood was significant. These types, if present in the main parts of the wood, did not flower at all unless they pushed above the hazels and so got more light. Otherwise it was only on the edges of the wood and by the sides of the rides that they formed blossoms. Sallow, on the other hand, bloomed well wherever it occurred, but it was an early-flowering type when no foliage was there to shadow it. The others were later in flowering and came in the shade phase. In the field layer, all were insect-pollinated except dog's mercury, and this again was exceptionally early-flowering.

Wind as a habitat factor is most effective in the tree and shrub layers, and it becomes less effective as a means of pollination as the foliage develops. It was, therefore, interesting to notice that hazel flowered long before the leaves developed and this was also true of ash and wych elm. The flowers of oak emerged at the same time as the leaves, but the foliage was by no means fully developed during the pollination phase. Dog's mercury was pollinated when no leaves were present on the shrubs and trees, and thus made use of the best period for this type of pollination.

When the insect-pollinated types were observed, it was noticeable that on sunny days in the pre-vernal stage there was a relatively large number of insects pollinating. Now the number of insects on the wing in March and April is much fewer than in May and June. However, in the latter months it was possible under comparable conditions to wait quite a long time before seeing a group of flowers visited. It was evident that the shade phase coincided with a drop in

the number of species of insects which visited the darker parts
of the wood : although by watching plants in the more open
spaces and rides it was obvious that there was no lack of
insects about.

In March and April honey bees (*Apis mellifica*) were often
seen. They were the chief pollinators of the wood anemone
which is a pollen flower, having no nectaries. They also
visited the earlier bluebells, ground ivy, strawberry and early
purple orchid. Bees are sometimes seen with tangled groups
of pollinia on their heads as a result. Later on they went to
dogrose and bramble, but these only flowered at the edges of
the wood or in rides.

The bee-fly (*Bombylius*) was an important pollinator of
primroses, and ground ivy and early bluebells, but they were
not seen after the shade phase had come. Sallow collected a
great variety of insects, as this provided one of the chief
supplies of nectar at this season. In the daytime, peacock
butterflies (*Nymphalis io*) fresh from hibernation were seen,
honey bees and bumble bees were also there and a host of
flies. At night on examination with a torch the golden eyes
of moths could be distinguished as they fed, often in large
numbers, on the nectar. These again were mainly hibernating
species such as common quaker (*Taeniocampa stabilis*), small
quaker (*Taeniocampa pulverulenta*), clouded drab (*Taeniocampa
incerta*) and satellite (*Eupsillia satellitia*).

The bugle flowers (*Ajuga reptans*) edging the rides of the
wood were visited by butterflies such as the pearl-bordered
fritillary (*Argynnis euphrosyne*) and bumble bees, while flies
were seen at the flowers of earthnut (*Conopodium majus*)
wood spurge (*Euphorbia amygdaloides*) and woodruff (*Asperula
odorata*).

It was interesting to try to investigate how the late-
flowering species overcame the difficulty of a reduced number
of insects. Butterfly orchid appeared to be adapted for moth
pollination with its white flowers which were relatively more
conspicuous at dusk than in daylight. Honeysuckle was also
visited by moths, and again the paler colour of the freshly-

opened, unpollinated flowers made them conspicuous. Both these flowers had a strong scent which was most evident at night.

In the daytime flies were seen visiting butterfly orchid and also twayblade, while butterflies visited spotted orchids at the edges of the paths.

It was generally concluded that the insects capable of pollinating the majority of flowers in the herb layer were not present in such large numbers at any season in the wood as outside, and that as shade increased the numbers became much fewer.

(6) *Seed Production*

It is another question whether the insect visits were sufficient to bring about adequate fertilization of the ovules. Two points had to be investigated in this connection—the average number of seeds formed per plant compared with those of the same species in more open situation, and the viability of those seeds.

There is much scope for further work along these lines, but as an example of the problem we can take the bluebell. A large number of samples were taken from the shaded part of the wood in July when the seeds were nearly ripe, and a similar lot obtained from an open region which had been coppiced. Counts were then made of the average number of capsules formed on each plant, and the number of seeds per capsule determined for each habitat. It was found that there was a greater number of capsules and seeds per capsule obtained from those in open situation. When, however, the seeds were sown, the percentage of germination did not differ very much in the two samples, though the total number of viable seeds was greater, of course, for those in the more open situation.

Perhaps the most interesting observation was that for the bluebells growing in the shaded parts of the wood, only the lower two or three capsules developed, although in the spring the number of flowers on the inflorescence was greater. This suggested that the later flowers to come out were not pollinated so well as the earlier ones. As the flowering period of the bluebell spreads from the light into the shade phase, it gives strong support to the theory that pollination by insects, except in certain very specialized species such as butterfly orchid, is very much less efficient during the shade phase.

Bluebell seeds, like those of many woodland plants, are rather large compared with those from plants of other habitats. This fits in with recent research which suggests that in the denser plant communities large seeds with their greater food supply enable the seedling to make quite a lot of growth before having to photosynthesize; thus in woodland plants it enables them to grow through the shade layer of competing herbaceous perennials and get to the light.

It would be most interesting to carry out further observation on all the more important members of the field layer to compare both average seed output and their reproductive capacity.

The average seed output is obtained by multiplying the average number of seeds per fruit with the average number of fruits per plant. Large numbers must be taken in each case for statistical purposes. If this figure is multiplied by the fraction of seeds that germinate (mean value) the average reproductive capacity is obtained.

Figures for average reproductive capacity when compared would give useful indication of the importance of seed production in the reproduction of woodland plants. Now, the reproductive capacity of bluebells living in a dense wood is low, and work on other plants such as dog's mercury and wood anemone suggest that it is likely to be true for the majority. If this is so, it would suggest that as the flora is almost entirely perennial, and as most of the perennating organs are also capable of vegetative reproduction, that the latter method is of great importance and probably of greater importance in a well-established community than that of seeds. This, however, would only apply to the spread of the species within the wood, not to colonizing new habitats.

In order to test the importance of the two methods of

reproduction it is possible to set up a number of permanent quadrats and to record from year to year any new plants. This was done by taking four wooden slats just over a metre long with holes bored at decimetre intervals. The four slats were bolted together near their ends so that a square metre was enclosed. String was then threaded across to corresponding holes, thus forming ten areas each of 10 square decimetres. The plants for each square were then plotted on graph paper to the scale of 10 : 1. If this is done for several years in succession (the position of the four corners being marked by white pegs) new plants may easily be noticed.

Observations showed that bluebell seedlings were not uncommon in the denser part but dog's mercury tended to spread vegetatively by means of underground rhizomes, new seedlings being rare. This tendency for dog's mercury to spread vegetatively under woodland conditions was emphasized by the association of whole patches of male plants together and then groups of female plants ; not a haphazard distribution as there would be through seed dispersal.

(7) *Fruit and Seed Dispersal Mechanisms*

Another important factor relating to the method of propagation is the efficiency of seed dispersal mechanisms. In the tree and shrub layer the most striking thing is that each member has an apparently excellent method of dispersal with some good structural adaptation of the fruit. Thus, the wind-dispersed species—ash, elm and sallow—all have fruits or seeds where the surface is increased considerably relative to the weight. The dominant plants, however, rely on great quantities of nuts which fall to the ground or are collected by squirrels or dormice. These animals may drop or bury them in different parts and forget where they have been stored.

Of the other shrubs, practically all have edible fruits which are dispersed by birds, but as they seldom fruited except at the edges of the wood and the borders of the rides it was largely a dispersal from outside to the interior of the wood. The very presence of these shrubs in the denser parts of the wood was good evidence of the success of the dispersal mechanism.

The most successful species in the shrub layer apart from hazel appeared to be honeysuckle, and its dispersal mechanism (berries eaten by birds) must be most efficient as great numbers of young plants were found in the field layer, many of which successfully found hazel branches for support in climbing to the light.

TABLE II

ADAPTATIONS TO REPRODUCTION
TREE AND SHRUB LAYER

SPECIES	VEGETATIVE REPRODUCTION	DISPERSAL ADAPTATION	AGENT
Oak . . .	None	Edible	Mammals, Birds
Ash . . .	None	Winged fruits	Wind
Wych Elm . .	*None	Winged fruits	Wind
Hazel . . .	None	Edible	Mammals
Sallow . .	None	Seeds with hairs	Wind
Maple . .	None	Winged fruits	Wind
Hawthorn . .	None	Edible	Birds
Privet . .	None	Edible	Birds
Holly . .	None	Edible	Birds
Spindle . .	None	Edible	Birds
Dogwood . .	None	Edible	Birds
Wayfaring tree .	None	Edible	Birds
Guelder rose .	None	Edible	Birds
Dog rose . .	*None	Edible	Birds
Blackberry .	Stolons	Edible	Birds, Mammals
Honeysuckle .	None	Edible	Birds
Black Bryony .	None	Edible	Birds

* Occasionally forms suckers, but of little significance in woods.

In the field layer the picture was very different. Here the majority of plants had no specialized means of dispersal of fruits or seeds. As far as could be ascertained, they just fell from the parent plant, dispersal being limited to a few inches. In contrast to this lack of specialization, however, there was usually a most efficient method of vegetative reproduction which was a further pointer towards the reliance on this method for normal reproduction within the wood.

A few plants were exceptional in having good dispersal methods. Enchanter's nightshade with its hooked fruits was dispersed by rabbits and other mammals including man. The same applied to burdock. In this case, however, as the plants in the denser parts seldom flowered it was again a dispersal from the open parts into the wood—another proof of its efficiency.

The other exceptions were the orchids with their fantastically small and light seeds which were adapted for wind dispersal even when winds were light.

Small pieces of evidence of dispersal efficiency can be collected by examining the fur of rabbits shot on the area, and any mammals found dead in the wood.

TABLE III
ADAPTATIONS TO REPRODUCTION
FIELD LAYER

SPECIES	VEGETATIVE REPRODUCTION	DISPERSAL ADAPTATION	AGENT
Ivy . . .	Rooting stems	* No fruits	None
Burdock . .	None	Hooked bracts	Mammals
Pendulous Sedge .	Rhizomes	None obvious	None
Fœtid Iris . .	Rhizomes	None? Edible?	?
Wood Anemone .	Rhizomes	None obvious	None
Bluebell . .	Bulbs	None obvious	None
Dog's Mercury .	Rhizomes	Soft prickles	Mammals?
Yellow Archangel .	Short creeping stems	None obvious	None
Lesser Celandine .	Root tubers, bulbils	None obvious	None
Primrose . .	None	None obvious	None
Cuckoo Pint . .	Corms	Edible	Birds
Goldilocks . .	None	None obvious	None
Violet . . .	Short rhizomes	Flicks out seeds	None
Bugle . . .	Runners	None obvious	None
Early Purple Orchid	None	Small and light	Wind
Spotted Orchid .	None	Small and light	Wind
Butterfly Orchid .	None	Small and light	Wind
Bird's Nest Orchid .	None	Small and light	Wind
Enchanter's Nightshade	Rooting stems	Hooked fruits	Mammals
Wood Spurge .	Rhizomes	None obvious	None
Woodruff . .	None	Hooked fruits	Mammals

* When in field layer.

CHAPTER IV

HABITAT FACTORS IN A WOOD

So far we have tried to describe some of the lines of enquiry followed out in order to discover some of the characteristics which are typical of plants living in woods. At this stage we begin to realize how the flora of a wood is no haphazard collection of plants, but each plant is present in the community because it has adapted successfully to the complex of habitat factors characteristic of a wood. We have already been brought up against some of these habitat factors such as light, and seen how the plants in the field layer are adapted to a light and shade phase, but it is time that these factors should be analysed in more detail so that further adaptations may be discovered.

The greatest difficulty in analysing habitat factors arises from the fact that in a complex environment they never act singly on a plant or animal, but always produce along with other factors a general set of conditions to which the organisms are adapted. To analyse them you have to separate the single factor from the complex, and it is easy to fall into the error of pinning down an adaptation to a particular factor instead of to the complex whole. Nevertheless, it is true that certain factors play a much greater part than others in affecting the lives of plants and animals, and by concentrating on these some progress may be made.

For a general survey of this kind it is not practicable to try to analyse all the climatic, edaphic (soil) and biotic (living) factors. It is more important to concentrate on those factors which appear to play a prominent part in the factor complex first ; of these, light would appear to be the most important.

(1) *Light*

There are several ways of measuring light intensity. A Watkins Bee Meter may be used with reasonable, but not very accurate results, the time taken for photographic paper to colour to a standard shade being inversely proportional to the intensity. However, for our study we used an Avo light meter which is a photoelectric instrument designed to measure intensity directly in foot candles. With this we compared the light intensity reaching the tree, shrub and field layer. As ultra-violet light is not utilized by a plant in photosynthesis we eliminated this part of the spectrum by placing a glass over the receiving surface. To increase the range of the instrument, marks were used to reduce the receiving area by a definite fraction. Days were chosen for the readings when there was a uniform blue sky, and when testing the light below the trees the instrument was always pointed in the same direction, and moved slowly backwards and forwards to eliminate error caused by flecks of sunlight coming through the leaves. As the light intensity differs from day to day, and from hour to hour, only the relative results were useful.

To take an example, the reading in the open was 3,600 foot candles, but below the tree canopy when fully developed the average reading was 240 foot candles. Under the shrub layer the average for area A was 27 foot candles, B 20 foot candles, and C 48 foot candles. The enormous reduction in light for the field layer during the shade phase was at once appreciated, and confirmed the belief that light intensity was of great importance. The changes in the three areas was interesting and appeared to be of some significance. Dog's mercury was absent from B which had the lowest average value, present in small patches in A, and dominant in C where much more light came through. Light could therefore be a factor in limiting its distribution, though other factors may also be important.

Special note was made of the numerous bare patches of ground in A and B, and the distribution of ivy. Average readings showed that if (on this day) the readings were 15 foot candles (0·42 per cent. of available light) or below, no vegetation occurred; if it rose to between 25 and 35 foot candles (0·70–0·97 per cent. of available light) ivy was dominant. It had previously been observed that ivy was the main dominant in A and B, but in C it was absent over most of the area, except around the base of the hazels. These regions were found to give lower readings than the areas between the shrubs.

There was, therefore, a strong pointer towards the conclusion that ivy could compete successfully for dominance when light intensities were low, but greater intensity tipped the balance in favour of dog's mercury and bluebells. Before a more definite conclusion could be reached, it would be necessary to take many more light readings in other woods to see if the same general pattern occurred.

Structural Adaptations to Light. Plants of the field layer were examined for structural adaptations that would enable the plant to make best use of what light was available for photosynthesis. It soon became evident that nearly all woodland plants displayed as much leaf surface as possible through leaf mosaic of one kind or another. The main methods can be exemplified by a small selection. Ivy, with its creeping stems and leaves filling in all available space and hardly overlapping, covered a very large area of the woodland floor. Bluebell, with its narrow leaves radiating out in all directions, with little overlap, formed almost a complete circle of leaf surface. Primrose, with its rosette of leaves again covered all the ground in the neighbourhood of the plants. This not only made use of all light available, but eliminated competition in the immediate vicinity.

It is generally true of plants that under poor light conditions the stems become more elongated and the leaf surface larger. This is particularly noticeable in woodland plants. Leaf surface of primroses were compared from different habitats— those in the main part of the wood and those in clearings of the same wood. The leaves were very much larger in the woodland plants, the difference being most marked in late May.

Burdock (*Arctium vulgare*) with its extremely large leaves, showed a different method of increasing surface, but with similar results to those obtained through leaf mosaic. Microscopic examination of the leaves of woodland plants shows that, on the whole, the dorsal cuticle tends to be thinner than in those plants which grow in more open situation, and the palisade cells are more elongated, but there are fewer layers of these cells.

(2) Humidity

It is clear that the humidity of the atmosphere is an important factor in determining the composition of plant communities. Any woodland area is evaporating into the air large quantities of water vapour, and the atmosphere inside the wood is heavily charged as a result. This has a most important effect on the soil, as far less water is evaporated from this surface when the humidity of the air is high. Add to this the sheltering effect of the trees, which also reduces evaporation, and it becomes clear that woodland plants compared with those in open situations have much less need to conserve their water by limiting transpiration. Thus many plants without special devices for restricting loss of water are able to live in woods and not in more exposed habitats.

To get some idea of the differences in evaporating power between different areas in the wood compared with outside, various experiments were carried out. The instrument used was an atmometer of the type designed by Dr. W. O. James and described in *An Introduction to Plant Ecology*, by A. G. Tansley. The whole instrument is filled with distilled water, and the rate of evaporation from the inverted porous pot measured by taking the mean time needed for a bubble introduced into the capillary tube to travel between two fixed points on the scale.

The most significant results were obtained on dry, still and sunny days. Several readings were taken at each of a number of situations in each area and it was found that there were marked differences. Area C showed the quickest rate of evaporation of the three main areas, but this (for example on a very dry day) was only 20 per cent. of the rate measured

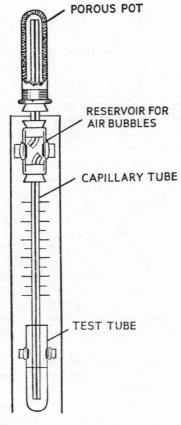

FIG. 6.   Atmometer of the type designed by Dr. W. O. James.

outside the wood. In A and B the rates were more or less comparable, and were about 15 per cent. of the outside figure.

(3) *Temperature*

Another factor of importance is temperature. Compared with that of the open pasture-land outside, woodland shows considerable differences. Due to the sun's rays being interrupted by the tree and shrub layer, and the evaporation of the water from the trees, the temperature during the day is much lower than outside, differences of up to 10° C. being recorded. On the other hand, the wood is sheltered from air currents to a large extent and consequently holds its heat longer than an open community, hence at night the temperatures are higher than outside. This variation can be measured by means of a number of maximum and minimum thermometers placed at different heights in the wood, and similarly outside by way of control.

The less extreme conditions of woodland compared with open communities make it an easier environment for the more delicate leaved plants, and along with the high humidity may be important in enabling a plant to live there.

(4) *Wind*

It is obvious that a wood acts as a wind break and consequently provides shelter for plants and animals living within it. This shelter will be greater near ground level and least in the tree layer. We have already seen that this shelter reduces evaporation rate both from the plants and soil surface, and is therefore bound up with the humidity of the air in producing conditions to which woodland plants are well adapted.

(5) *Soil*

The part played by soil conditions in determining the characteristics of the flora and fauna cannot be overemphasized. But the soil itself is such a complex of factors that it is extremely difficult to get anything more than a vague picture of its effects.

The Thurlbear woods are situated on an outcrop of Lower Lias, and the flora of the whole wood was typically a calcareous one. One might mention especially the presence of Wayfaring tree (*Viburnum lantana*), Dogwood (*Cornus sanguinea*), Spindle (*Euonymus europaeus*) and Clematis (*Clematis vitalba*) as typical calcicoles in the shrub layer. Particular note was made of any differences in soil characters in the three main areas, to see if these were in any way connected with the distribution of the dominants.

The soil analysis* was carried out as follows: In each main area of the wood a small pit was dug with a sharp spade so that a clean-cut vertical section was visible about 9 inches deep. As the soil was mainly clay the earth did not fall in. This gave a soil profile which was then sketched to show the variation with depth and the rooting systems. It was found to be possible to remove a complete vertical slice of this soil for analysis.

For a general analysis the samples used were obtained by mixing portions from different depths ranging from 1 to 6 inches. This cut out the main layer of organic debris on the surface. Plant roots were also removed. It was also interesting to compare samples taken from the surface, 2 inches down, and 6 inches down to see what differences there were, as it was possible that variation might be related to the rooting depths of the various plants present.

The samples were then brought back to the laboratory and analysed. To get some idea of texture, air-dried samples were weighed and passed through sieves of different standard meshes and the residues on each sieve weighed. The results were expressed as follows:—

Percentage of particles larger than	2 mm.	= gravel.
,,	,, 2 to 0·2 mm.	= coarse sand.
,,	,, 0·2 to 0·02 mm.	= fine sand.
,,	,, 0·02 to 0·002 mm.	= silt.
,,	,, below 0·002 mm.	= clay.

* For detailed description of soil analysis text-books should be consulted, e.g. McLean and Cook (see Bibliography).

The soil was also analysed for available water by air-drying weighed samples until weight was constant. The air-dried soil was then placed in a steam oven until there was no further loss in weight, the difference being the capillary water still present in the soil after air-drying. To estimate the humus content the oven-dried soil was then burned on metal trays until the humus was all burned away and no further loss in weight occurred. The residue was the inorganic material present.

The pH of the soil samples was determined by shaking up some soil with distilled water and using a B.D.H. capillator with universal indicator. Very clean glassware had to be used, but new test tubes were found to be useless until well washed as they gave a strong alkaline reaction.

Free calcium carbonate was tested for by adding dilute hydrochloric acid and noticing if effervescence occurred.

Results showed that the soil texture was a stiff clay in all parts, but it was slightly more crumbly in C due to an increase in the percentage of fine and coarse sand particles. Free calcium carbonate was present in soil samples from C, but very little could be detected at A, and none at all at B. It was noticed that the amount of calcium carbonate at C increased with soil depth.

The pH of the areas showed that C was highest ranging from 7·3 to 7·8 ; a slightly alkaline reaction correlated with the presence of free calcium carbonate. In other parts of the wood the soil was slightly acid, ranging from 6·0 to 6·9.

The following tables give further details :—

TABLE IV

ANALYSIS OF SOIL SAMPLES FROM THE THREE MAIN AREAS (JUNE)

(Per cent. figures are averages of several samples)

	AREA A	AREA B	AREA C
Available water . .	26·9%	19·1%	23·5%
*Capillary water . .	4·0%	4·4%	6·2%
*Humus . . .	8·6%	7·8%	7·6%
*Inorganic residue . .	87·4%	87·8%	86·2%
pH	6·5–6·9	6·0–6·8	7·3–7·8
Free calcium carbonate .	A few particles	Absent	Present

* Given as percentage of air-dried soil.

Table V

Soil Analyses of Areas B and C to show Variation with Depth

B (ANEMONE-BLUEBELL SOCIETY)				C (DOG'S MERCURY-BLUEBELL SOCIETY)		
Surface layer	2 in. depth	6 in. depth		Surface layer	2 in. depth	6 in. depth
21%	13%	18·5%	Available water . .	31·2%	5·2%	18·6%
16%	10%	5·7%	*Capillary water . .	14·5%	8·7%	6·7%
11·7%	4·3%	5·2%	*Humus . . .	20·0%	6·3%	8·3%
72·3%	85·7%	89·1%	*Inorganic residue .	65·5%	85·0%	85·0%
			Free calcium carbonate .	Slight	Moderate	Considerable
6·8	6·8	6·0	pH	7·3	7·8	7·5

The water table was well below the surface in C, but in certain parts of A and B there were regions where it reached the surface. Here the water remained in the cart tracks right through the summer, and gave rise to an entirely different society of plants. These wet regions were dominated in the field layer by pendulous sedge (*Carex pendula*), with a number of sallows in the shrub layer. Other typical plants included *Juncus conglomeratus*, mint (*Mentha aquatica*), figwort (*Scrophularia aquatica*), fœtid iris (*Iris foetidissima*), and in the wettest places a species of *Callitriche*.

This *Carex pendula* society illustrated very well the effect of increased water content of the soil on the flora, as the same species were met with in isolated patches of the wood wherever the soil was saturated for most of the year.

(6) Biotic Factors

Under this heading we group the effects on the plant community of any other living organisms. In a sense, all the animals in a wood exert an influence on the plants, but for purposes of convenience, the inter-relationships between vegetarian types and the flora will be discussed later on. There are, however, certain organisms which may by their

* Given as percentage of air-dried soil.

single action have a profound effect on the floral composition and structure of the wood, and these will be mentioned here.

Man himself exerts a tremendous influence in this respect by coppicing and felling. Opportunities for studying the effect of the former occurred in a portion of the wood near A where oaks were absent. This area was dominated by hazels in the shrub layer, and coppicing of part of the area took place in the winter of 1948–49. Shade was very considerable before this occurred, as the hazels were close together and formed a thick canopy. Although in the pre-vernal and vernal periods the herb layer was fairly well developed, the shade cast in summer and autumn caused the remaining plants to be straggly and somewhat etiolated. By marking out permanent quadrats in this area it was possible to see the change in composition after coppicing had taken place.

During the first summer the existing perennials made good growth, flowering being rather more conspicuous than on the uncut area. The presence of a large number of annuals was a most obvious feature during the spring and summer ; these had presumably seeded from other areas. It was not determined whether the seeds had been dormant in the woodland soil for some time and germinated when the conditions were changed due to coppicing, or whether seeding had occurred later and owing to comparative lack of competition had led effective colonization. Thus large areas of field penny-cress (*Thlaspi arvense*) made their appearance and common forget-me-not (*Myosotis arvensis*) became abundant. A number of other weeds of arable land occurred.

During the second year—that is to say, just over a year after coppicing, the appearance of the area was much altered in the pre-vernal aspect by a great increase in flowering of the normal woodland perennials. This was most marked in the cases of the primrose, violet, barren strawberry and strawberry. It is thought that this may be due to greater photosynthesis leading to an increase in the carbon-nitrogen ratio, and this affects flowering. The hazels made rapid growth during this summer and once more started to have an important shading effect.

THURLBEAR

Quadrat I   27:3:50   *Imetre X Imetre*

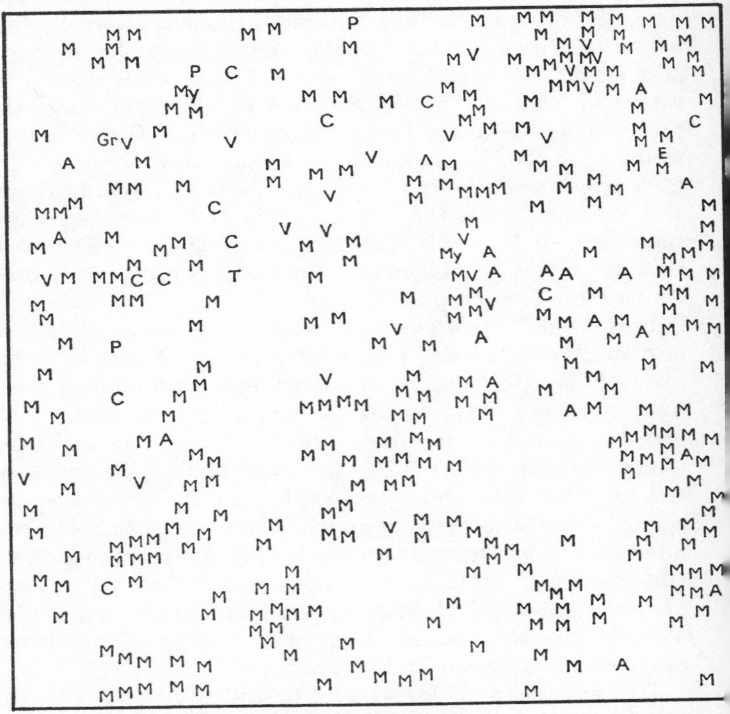

SYSTEM OF NAMING

M Mercurialis perennis   P Primula vulgaris
Cr Crataegus monogyna   A Arum maculatum
T Taraxacum officinale   V Viola riviniana
E Euonymus europaeus   My Myosotis Sp.
            C Cardamine hirsuta

FIG. 7.   Quadrat from Coppiced Area.

This was noticeable in its result the following year when the annuals were much reduced in number, and the flowering, though good, was not so pronounced as for the year before.

Oaks had been felled in other parts of the wood, allowing more light to penetrate to the shrub layer. This increased in size until it had a very considerable shading effect on the herb layer.

Various mammals have an important effect on the woodland flora. It was noted that in the vicinity of rabbit warrens and a badger set, nettles and elders became prominent members of the field and shrub layers respectively. In well-established badger sets and rabbit warrens in woods, this is often most marked, but in Thurlbear the effect was only slight. We have shown elsewhere * that the constant shifting of the earth due to burrowing of rabbits and badgers restricts the number of plants that are able to colonize it, and that nettles and elders flourish because they are distasteful, while the others are eaten off as young plants by the badgers and rabbits. Thus the presence of nettles and elders in these areas is the direct result of badger and rabbit activity.

It is also well known that rabbits, wood mice and voles have an important influence on the herb layer. Although large numbers of tree seedlings may develop, they are usually eaten off before they reach a reasonable size, thus preventing natural regeneration of deciduous woods. It is only when there is a year when enormous numbers of acorns or beech mast are formed that the seedlings get a chance, and then probably only if it coincides with a low point in the rodent cycle of numbers.

Interesting experiments can be set up to illustrate the effect of these rodents on the flora by fencing off small areas with strong wire netting of varying meshes—some small enough to keep out voles and mice, and others larger to exclude rabbits but not the smaller mammals. The wire has to be let into the ground at least 6 inches to prevent burrowing, and in lighter soils it should be deeper.

Certain fungi should be mentioned as important biotic

* Neal, E. *The Badger* (Collins. The New Naturalist Series).

factors. The work of the normal saprophytes will be mentioned when the general food cycle is discussed, but the mycorrhizal fungi play a special part. Little practical work can be done without specialized knowledge and technique to show the importance of these soil fungi, but it is certain that for some of the trees and herbs their presence is essential. Some are endotrophic in their action, living partly within the cells of the root and partly in the soil. They are thus able to act as saprophytes and pass on some of the digested material to the plant with which they are associated. This is true of many of the orchids, the bird's nest orchid, for example, having lost practically all its chlorophyll is completely dependent upon its mycorrhizal fungus for nutrition. Sections of the root of this orchid when examined under the microscope showed the characteristic hyphæ within the cortical cells.

A large number of other plants including many woodland trees have ectotrophic mycorrhiza associated with them. These form a matted mycelium round the tiny roots and act like root hairs in passing on water and probably other material to the trees.

Other important associations between different species of plants are the lichens. These dual organisms, composed of fungal and algal elements, can usually only exist in their specialized habitats by living in symbiosis. Thus the lichens on the tree trunks rely on the fungus partner for protection, water absorption and retention, while the algæ carry out photosynthesis and provide organic food for the fungus.

CHAPTER V

THE FOOD CYCLE

Now that we have built up a picture of the floral scaffolding of the wood, we can attempt to show some of the characteristics of the fauna and the inter-relationships of the animal types.

Animals are entirely dependent upon plants for their existence, either directly through the food they eat, or indirectly through other animals which in their turn are vegetarians. This fundamental relationship between animals and plants is due to the lack of chlorophyll in animals. Unlike green plants, they are unable to synthesize complex organic substances such as proteins and carbohydrates from simple substances in the environment like carbon dioxide, water and salts. They are thus dependent upon green plants for the compounds which are essential for their growth and for the liberation of energy for vital purposes.

In every large community there are well-defined groups of animals which are inter-related in a very definite way. The basic group is comprised of vegetarians. These may vary from the aphids on the oak leaves to the deer that browse the vegetation. They vary enormously both in structure and biological position in the community, but the majority are beautifully adapted to the different plants or parts of plants on which they feed.

The vegetarians provide the food for the next large group, the carnivores. These again vary very much in size and in feeding habits. Some may be small like the predaceous insects, which are themselves the food of insectivorous birds, and these in turn may be the prey of larger carnivores. The largest carnivores seldom have any enemies other than man, and thus are at the end of their food chain except for parasites.

A third important group comprises the scavengers. These feed on dead material or the waste products of animals, and partly account for the fact that dead animals are so seldom seen.

The fourth category of animals includes the parasites. These live in or on the bodies of other organisms and are completely dependent upon them for their sustenance. They may feed on the living tissues, or on the food of their host in the case of intestinal parasites.

Thus all the time there is a continual utilization of material

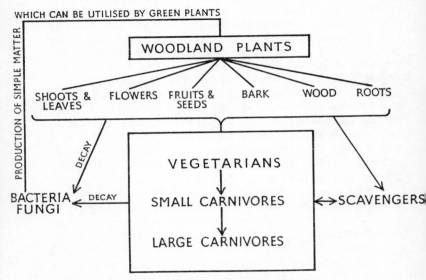

FIG. 8. The Food Cycle in a Wood.

originally made by green plants. This would quickly lead to a depletion of the essential basic substances if it were not for the fact that there were organisms at work replacing them. These are the saprophytes—plants having no chlorophyll which bring about decay. They consist of bacteria and fungi which, by a series of reactions involving a chain of different species, break down the complex substances into carbon dioxide, water and simple salts which can be utilized once more by green plants.

There is therefore a food cycle in every large community composed of well-defined groups of organisms, all related to each other according to their manner of feeding and all dependent upon one another. This is shown as a diagram in Fig. 8.

With this fundamental picture in mind, it was our aim to apply it to Thurlbear woods and fill in the details as far as possible. Obviously the first thing to do was to list as many as possible of the animals in the community, finding out at the same time the method of feeding, the nature of the habitat, and any adaptations we could discover.

CHAPTER VI

THE MAIN ANIMAL HABITATS

IT was necessary at this stage to divide up the wood into its main microhabitats and to devise methods for finding the animal population of each. This had obviously to be based upon the primary floral divisions of tree layer, shrub layer, field layer and moss layer, but some of these could usefully be subdivided. How far these habitats should be subdivided was difficult to determine, as they ranged in type from the complete tree as an ecological unit to small rain puddles in the saddle of a tree in which leaves, bacteria, ciliates and mosquito larvæ were present. The smaller the subdivisions, however, the greater the overlap between the species inhabiting them, and it was found in practice that it was not useful at this stage to subdivide too much.

The scheme we used was as follows :—

(1) Tree layer according to species of tree.

    (*a*) Leaves, buds and shoots.

    (*b*) Trunks and boughs.

        (i) On surface among mosses and lichens.

        (ii) In the actual wood (*a*) of living trees.

                          (*b*) of dead trees.

        (iii) Under the bark of living or dead trees.

    (*c*) At or in the roots.

    (*d*) In fruits or seeds.

(2) Shrub layer according to species, as for tree layer where applicable.

(3) Field layer according to species, with special reference to dominants.

(4) Moss and leaf-litter layer.

(5) In the soil.

CHAPTER VII

METHODS OF FINDING WOODLAND ANIMALS

ANIMALS are on the whole active creatures and tend to move from one habitat to another, and the larger the animal the greater the movement as a rule. It therefore became obvious that the method of searching microhabitats for their characteristic fauna was much more applicable to small species such as insects, than to the mammals and birds. It was found in practice that it was easier for the larger animals to be studied according to species, and by constant observation to determine the general habitat for which they showed preference, rather than the other way about.

The whole concept of a preference habitat is an important one. Numerical work soon shows that, although a species may be found in a number of different habitats, it is usually found in much larger numbers, or more often, in one. This preference habitat is the one to which it is best adapted. For some species which are highly specialized (such as some of the parasites or wood borers) there is only one possible habitat. Others, which are less specialized, may be found in various habitats. Counting is often the only way to discover the preferential habitats of some species such as birds.

The birds when seen were listed according to species. It was soon noticed that these had definite preference habitats both in relation to feeding and nesting, and that these were not necessarily the same for a species. Thus, while feeding, the blue tits would keep to the tree canopy, but they would nest in any suitable hole ; and blackbirds would feed amongst the leaf litter, but would nest in the shrub layer.

For the study of the smaller inhabitants of various microhabitats, special techniques were employed to suit the various conditions. For the fauna of the leaves, buds and shoots of the tree and shrub layer, two methods were used. The more laborious but more valuable way was to examine the shoots *in situ* with great care. In this manner we were able to see the animals in their natural positions and observe what they were doing ; this was specially valuable when noting their feeding habits. An easier and quicker method was to use a beating tray. This in principle is any kind of receptacle from a sheet to an umbrella which is held under a bough, which is then sharply knocked with a stout stick. The majority of the animals on the shoot are dislodged and fall on to the tray, and can be examined.

Various types of beating tray are on the market, such as the Bignell tray, but it is very easy to improvise a suitable piece of apparatus :—

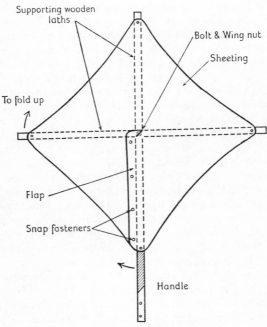

Supporting wooden laths

Bolt & Wing nut

Sheeting

To fold up

Flap

Snap fasteners

Handle

FIG. 9.   Beating Tray.

The animals living among the mosses and lichens on a tree trunk are not numerous and are often difficult to find. A number of species merely rest there for short or long periods between bouts of activity. Thus numerous flies were to be seen basking in the sunshine, and night-flying moths were occasionally discovered motionless and flat against the bark. The smaller animals were best found by stripping off samples of the mosses and lichens and examining them on a white sheet. These included some of the caterpillars which are lichen feeders, such as those of the common footman moth (*Lithosia lurideola*). The smallest inhabitants were discovered by using a Berlese funnel, described later.

The wood-borers are difficult to collect from living trees though their exit holes may be obvious, and in the case of the goat moth (*Cossus cossus*) the species can be identified with certainty by the smell alone. In rotting stumps the inhabitants are easier to find as the wood can be broken up to expose the inmates. These were found to vary somewhat according to the degree of rottenness of the wood, its dampness, situation, and also according to the species of tree—these points were noted when collecting material from such habitats.

The under-bark community can only be discovered by peeling off the bark when this is loose. Again we found it most important not only to note the type of tree, but also the distribution of the animals in relation to moisture and degree of exposure, for example, whether from the upper or under side of a felled trunk.

Tree-root feeders are not numerous in woodland, the most characteristic being the larvæ of the ghost swift (*Hepialus humuli*) which occasionally penetrate the pith region of young oak roots ; these, however, are not often discovered unless damage is considerable, and then it is usually only noticeable in young saplings.

Animals living on fruits and seeds may be found in a number of ways. Beating ash or elm fruits when still green and soft was found to be profitable, and revealed certain caterpillars such as those of the brick moth (*Agrochola circellaris*). Sallow fruits are also the food of many insects, including weevils and lepidopterous larvæ. Some of the larger ones were discovered by beating, but others were found by picking large numbers of the fruits and keeping them in a box

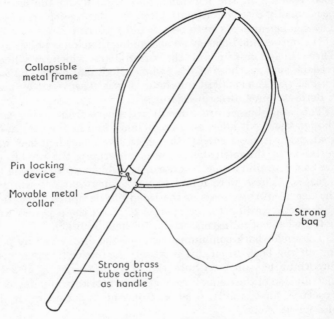

Collapsible metal frame

Pin locking device

Movable metal collar

Strong bag

Strong brass tube acting as handle

FIG. 10.   Sweeping Net.

until the adults emerged, as the latter were more easily identified.

The inhabitants of the field layer could to some extent be found by searching the different plants, especially the dominants, but far more were found by sweeping. A sweeping net is rather like a specially strengthened butterfly net. It can be used by pushing it through the plants like a shrimping net, or from above by sweeping movements. A proportion of the animals will fall into the vegetation, but with practice you soon learn to alter your technique according to the type of flora you are sweeping.

The sweeping net has disadvantages which have to be taken into account. Unless the field layer is composed of one type of plant you collect indiscriminately from any that are present. In woodland it is only in certain areas, such as where dog's mercury is dominant, that you can be reasonably certain that you are sweeping from that plant alone ; but when used with care the disadvantages can be reduced to a minimum. The catch should be examined frequently, because the animals may get mixed up with a lot of debris and may easily become damaged.

Sweeping can also be carried out with profit at night, because there are a number of forms which lie during the day near the roots, but at night climb up to the leaves to feed; these include a number of moth larvæ, especially noctuids.

The moss and leaf litter layer contains a large number of forms which are not at all easy to see. We found the best method was to rake together large quantities of this debris, and put it in a sack for transport. This could then be examined at our leisure. Small quantities of this material were then placed in a coarse-mesh sieve and shaken over white paper. We found it useful to hang a 100-watt lamp just above the sieve as most of the animals in leaf litter are negatively photo- tactic. As the animals passed through the sieve they were easily seen and collected. Most of the inhabitants are very subject to drying up—this is specially true of gill-breathing forms like the woodlice, so they were kept according to species in different petri-dishes lined by wet filter papers. We found it profitable to take samples of leaf litter from the wood at different times of the year, because there is considerable variation in the number of species present at different seasons.

Very minute forms were found by putting small quantities of the litter into a Berlese funnel. This consists of a large funnel (into which the litter is placed) above which is sus- pended a 100-watt bulb. The animals tend to go away from

the light and heat from the bulb, and towards greater
humidity, and pass down the tube of the funnel into a dish of
water placed below from which they can be collected. A more
efficient form of apparatus has a water jacket round the funnel
into which hot water can be put, thereby heating the material
more effectively.

Some of the more active animals that inhabit the ground

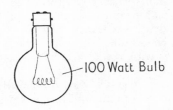

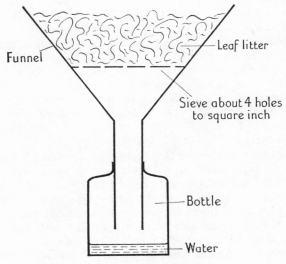

FIG. 11.   Berlese Funnel.

layer are not collected easily by these methods and special techniques had to be employed. Small jam jars sunk up to the rim in soil were found to be effective for trapping some of the larger predaceous insects, and if they were baited they were more effective. By putting in pieces of meat or a dead animal, for example, carrion beetles were easily caught in this way. Millipedes were collected in numbers by putting pieces of raw potato under damp sacking on the ground.

Small mammals such as wood mice and voles can best be caught by trapping. The best type for this purpose is the small mammal trap made by Longworths of Oxford. This is placed in the runs and lined with moss, and baited. The animals by an ingenious device shut the trap once they are inside and cannot get out ; they are unhurt, but the traps should be examined every twenty-four hours as small mammals quickly die of starvation.

Two methods were used to discover the animals inhabiting the soil. The first was to clear an area about a yard square of surface vegetation or leaf litter, and then pour on a solution of potassium permanganate in water (7 gm. to 2 gallons water). The worm population soon wriggle up to the surface and can be collected. This method is most successful when the soil is wet. The second method was by flotation. A sample of the earth was taken and broken up in water, and left to soak. The larger animals come to the surface at once, but the smaller ones may be some time before they become released from the earth particles. It was sometimes found to be useful to add a few drops of iso-butyl alcohol to the water to disperse the foam, this made observation of the smaller animals easier.

There are, of course, a number of types which in the daytime are more often seen on the wing than at rest, these include some of the butterflies, dragonflies and various hymenoptera. These were captured by means of a butterfly net.

Dung provides a specialized habitat for a number of species, mainly beetles and flies. Many of these may not be visible on the surface, but if the dung were placed in a bucket of water they soon floated to the top and could be removed.

CHAPTER VIII

FOOD RELATIONSHIPS

(1) *Biological Niches and Food Chains*

HAVING found ways and means of discovering the animals in their various habitats it was our aim to find out as much as possible about their inter-relationships and adaptations. It has been said that an animal has three main purposes in life— seeking food, reproducing its kind and self-preservation. By concentrating on the ways in which these purposes were achieved in as many types as possible, a much bigger picture of the whole woodland community was obtained. Of these the method of feeding was the most fundamental as it was this activity that linked the types together more completely than any other. Our main concern was therefore to find out as much as possible of the feeding habits of these animals and so build up some of the food chains in the community.

It was useful at this stage to use a classification of feeding habits so that any type we found could be put into its right place. We used for this purpose a classification used by Imms for insects which we adapted to suit all the animals we came across. This was as follows :—

Vegetarians
(1) LEAF, BUD AND SHOOT FEEDERS
     (a) *Defoliators*   *e.g.* Caterpillars.
                                       Snails and slugs.
                                       Rabbits, mice, voles, deer.
     (b) *Miners*   *e.g.* Caterpillars.
(2) SUCKERS OF PLANT JUICES
     (a) *Sap feeders*   *e.g.* Aphids, bugs, frog hoppers.
     (b) *Nectar feeders*   *e.g.* Butterflies, moths, bees, flies.
(3) FRUIT AND SEED FEEDERS   *e.g.* Weevils, caterpillars.
                                         e.g. Wood mouse, vole, badger.
                                         e.g. Nuthatch, chaffinch, thrush.
(4) GALL FORMERS   *e.g.* Gall wasps, gall midges.
(5) BARK FEEDERS   *e.g.* Bark beetles.
                                         e.g. Wood lice.
                                         e.g. Millipedes.
                                         e.g. Grey squirrel, rabbits.

(6) WOOD BORERS   *e.g.* Wood wasp, moth larvæ, beetle larvæ.

(7) ROOT FEEDERS   *e.g.* Moth larvæ, beetle larvæ.

(8) FUNGUS FEEDERS   *e.g.* Beetles, fly larvæ, springtails.

Carnivores

(1) PREDATORS   *e.g.* Ladybirds, lacewing larvæ, syrphid larvæ, beetles.

     e.g. Centipedes.

     e.g. Insect eating, mollusc, and worm eating, large carnivores.

     e.g. Fox, badger, stoat, hedgehog.

(2) BLOOD SUCKERS   *e.g.* Mosquitoes, flies.

     e.g. Spiders.

(3) PARASITES   *e.g.* Fleas, ticks, ichneumons, chalcid wasps, tachinid flies.

Omnivores   *e.g.* Badger.

Scavengers

(1) FEEDERS ON SUBSTANCES OF VEGETABLE ORIGIN

     e.g. Springtails.

     e.g. Earthworms.

     e.g. Mites.

(2) FEEDERS ON SUBSTANCES OF ANIMAL ORIGIN

     (*a*) *Dung feeders*   *e.g.* Flies and their larvæ, beetles.

     (*b*) *Carrion feeders*   *e.g.* Fly larvæ, beetles.

This classification of feeding habits brings out the principle of the biological niche. This term is used to denote the position of the animal in a community in relation to the other members, especially in terms of its feeding habits. The term can be used to include a large group of animals like the carnivores, or more usefully be sub-divided into smaller niches according to the type of food or the size of the animal. Thus the defoliators can be sub-divided into the insects with biting mouth-parts such as caterpillars, the molluscs which scrape the vegetation by means of a radula, for example the slugs and snails, and the mammals which bite off the leaves with their teeth. In each of these categories there is a difference in method of feeding and a difference in the size of the animal. These differences of size are very important as a means of separating animals into different niches, because size often determines the type of animal that is able to prey upon them. Thus the carnivorous insects may be able to prey upon caterpillars, but not on slugs or snails, while some birds may be able to feed on slugs but not on rabbits.

Some niches were seen to be of greater importance than others in woodland, as the animals that filled them formed the food of a large number of other animals. Thus the aphids living on the sap of the oak leaves in astronomical numbers provided the main food of numerous birds, and carnivorous insects. Ladybirds and their larvæ took large numbers with methodical precision, while certain pentatomid bugs also fed upon them, piercing them with their rostra and sucking them dry in quick succession. Hoverfly larvæ also destroyed vast numbers, and the larvæ of lacewings took their toll. But insects were not the only animals to feed on aphids ; insectivorous birds such as bluetits ate large numbers, and during the winter when food was scarce, aphid eggs are said to feature prominently in their diet. Thus aphids provide one of the " key industries " (as Elton describes them) of the woodland community.

The springtails in the top soil and leaf litter formed a corresponding key industry in a different habitat, and provided food for predaceous insects such as ground beetles, caterpillars and insectivorous birds which routed amongst the litter.

Thus these two key industries soon led us to other important niches—that of the carnivorous insects and birds. Both comprised numerous species which were specialized in various ways to feed on slightly different foods, or in different habitats.

It soon became evident that these niches formed important links between one type and another, and some of these food chains could be determined. Thus the aphids which fed on the plant sap were fed upon by ladybirds and syrphid larvæ, which in their turn were preyed upon by insectivorous birds such as warblers, which formed the main food of the large carnivorous birds such as sparrow hawks (of which one pair only was seen in the wood).

The small defoliators such as caterpillars formed the food for numerous birds. This was especially noticeable during the nesting season when it was possible, by watching from a hide near the nest, to see the food brought to the young. Robins and tits brought in large numbers of larvæ, the former from the low herbage or shrubs, the latter from the trees. It was interesting to note how the size of the larvæ differed with the development of the young birds. It appeared that for most species the moth eggs mainly hatched as the buds were bursting ; by the time the young birds had hatched the larvæ were big enough to be their food, and as they grew they kept pace with the bird development to give them larger and more satisfying mouthfuls ! If the times had been thrown out of gear and the birds nested too soon, or the insects hatched too late, difficulties of feeding might have been acute. This was one striking instance of the interdependence of animal types in terms of time, and the importance of synchronization.

Other defoliators such as slugs and snails were eaten by birds, often of different species although there was obviously much overlap. Thus blackbirds were prominent in this respect, routing among the leaf litter for these molluscs.

All these birds of small or intermediate size were the prey of the sparrow hawks.

Larger defoliators such as rabbits, which were seen feeding on the foliage of the field layer and on the newly-fallen leaves from the trees, were preyed upon by foxes. Badgers did not eat the adults, but young rabbits in the nest were discovered by scent and eaten whole. The badgers would not enlarge the entrance to the nest, but would dig vertically downwards to reach the young by the shortest route. Buzzards would also eat rabbits, but only if they strayed out of the wood on to the more open parts.

In working out the food chains, we found it convenient to start with a specialized part of the plant community such as the leaves, wood or fruits and find out what types were feeding on them, working up to the larger carnivores which always stood at the head of the food chain. Thus the main food chains based on the leaf-eaters can be shown diagrammatically in Fig. 12.

The woody parts of the trees formed the food of various wood-boring insects, these were mainly beetle larvæ and the caterpillars of certain moths. These became the food of insectivorous birds of more specialized habits, of which the greater spotted woodpecker (*Dryobates major*) was the chief example in Thurlbear wood.

The flowers provided pollen and nectar for various species of

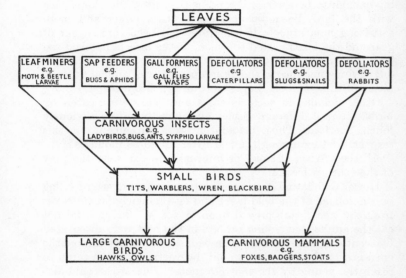

FIG. 12. Food Chains on Leaf-eaters.

insects; bees visited them for both substances, flies and butterflies for the nectar only. Beetles, on the other hand, according to species, fed on any part of the flower, biting the petals or stamens as well as feeding on the nectar. These in turn formed the food of the birds and so to the large carnivores once more.

Fruit and seed-eaters told the same story. Whether they were the larvæ of lepidoptera or weevil beetles, they formed the food of the smaller birds, or else seed-eating birds would eat them incidentally. The latter was true of such types as chaffinch, bullfinch, nuthatch, mistle thrush, wood pigeon and pheasant. These again led to the large carnivores, the smaller ones to the hawks and owls, the larger ground nesting types such as the pheasant, to the fox.

An important niche in the woodland community was filled

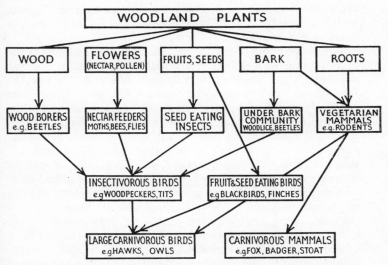

FIG. 13. Food Chains based on Vegetarians other than Leaf-eaters.

by the small vegetarian rodents, the main species discovered at Thurlbear being the wood mouse (*Apodemus sylvaticus*) and the short-tailed vole (*Microtus agrestis*). Both feed on various kinds of vegetable matter from the shoots to the roots and bark. Seeds are also a favourite diet of the wood mouse, the remains of acorns and hazel nuts witnessing to their activity. These rodents form an important part of the diet of carnivorous birds and mammals. Owls and hawks feed on the wood mice at night and foxes eat large numbers when other food is scarce or when the mice are particularly numerous. Badgers will also eat them.

Some of these food chains may be illustrated diagrammatically as in Fig. 13.

All these food chain diagrams are, of course, great simplifications of what takes place. Although the main steps are true, there are so many side chains and variations that no diagram which attempted all the detail could be made for such a complex community.

It was one thing to get a generalized idea of the foods of the more prominent members of a woodland community ; it was another thing altogether to get exact information about the food of any of the more indiscriminate feeders. This applied especially to the larger carnivores such as mammals and birds, and was only attempted for a few types. The food of mammals and birds can be determined by three main methods ; observation of the animals while feeding, stomach analysis and dung analysis. The first method was found most useful for diurnal creatures, especially birds, although the food had to be of reasonable size to be recognized. Stomach analysis was the most exact method, but material was seldom obtained for the purpose. Dung analysis when carried out systematically over a long period gave good results in some instances, but no trace of softer animal foods remained.

Analysis of badger dung was attempted as the badgers used special pits near the sets in which they deposited their dung ; this made systematic collection easier. The technique used was to put a little at a time through a gravy strainer, washing it continuously with a stream of water until the residue was quite clean. This was then put in a white dish containing water and examined. In this way vegetable remains became apparent, insect skins became recognizable and larger structures such as bones, fur or beetle elytra became obvious. Microscopic examination was sometimes found to be helpful, especially for things like the chætæ of worms. The same method can be used for fox dung when discovered. Rather similar work on owl pellets was attempted for the brown owl,

TABLE VI
BADGER DUNG ANALYSES

DATE	MATERIAL
Oct. 10th	Grass and other vegetable remains. Some thin flaky bark from some tree or shrub.
Oct. 26th	Fibrous vegetable material. Some grass. One noctuid larva.
Nov. 15th	Almost entirely vegetable material—mainly grass, but also a large number of black angular seeds resembling leek seeds. A few insect remains too broken for identification.
Dec. 23rd	Mainly vegetable matter of a fibrous nature, but including a lot of grass. One lepidopterous larva of the Hepialus type. One large Staphylinid larva. One earwig. One dor-beetle (*Geotrupes sp.*).
Dec. 31st	*Staphylinus olens* larva. Much hair of adult rabbit. Broken pieces of rabbit bone. Many fibrous roots. Some grass. Several large leaves.
Jan. 3rd	Mainly leaves broken up into small pieces—not indentified. Grass in fair proportion. Fibrous roots. Remains of four beetles—one *Geotrupes* and three ground beetles.
Jan. 6th	Mainly vegetable material, much of it fibrous. Some grass. Small pieces of leaves. Earthworm chætæ.
Jan. 10th	Fragments of several *Geotrupes* and a number of smaller ground beetles. One noctuid larva. Much grass. Leaves in small fragments.
Feb. 4th	Almost entirely vegetable material including fibrous roots, grass and leaves.
Feb. 14th	Mainly vegetable material.
Feb. 28th	Much remains of adult rabbit—bones and fur. The bones were all broken up into small pieces. Quite a lot of vegetable matter.
March 1st	Fibrous plant material, a few beetle elytra (*Geotrupes*) and several ground beetles. Rabbit fur (from adult).
March 4th	Fibrous plant material only.

the pellets were dissected, after soaking for twenty-four hours in water, and the contents analysed.

(2) *Food Chains Involving Saprophytes and Scavengers*

So far the only food chains mentioned have been those which arose directly from living vegetable matter in the wood. There are, however, supplementary food chains which are derived from the dead remains of plants and animals. We found it convenient to separate this dead organic matter into dead plants, dead animals, and dung, as the organisms that were feeding on these materials tended to be of different types. It soon became evident, however, that although this was a useful device, there was inevitably some overlap and that many types fed on dead organic matter indiscriminately whether of plant or animal origin.

We have already briefly alluded to the essential work carried out by saprophytes such as bacteria and fungi in the general food cycle in a woodland community. By their activity organic material is once more made available to plants for further synthesis into carbohydrates, proteins and fats. These saprophytes, however, are the food of numerous types of animals and thus give rise to food chains of the kind already described. Thus the fungi may be eaten by a number of different animals. Slugs were found to eat many of the larger basidiomycetes some of which are poisonous to mammals. When the heads of the fungi were broken open it was not unusual to find the larvæ of certain diptera and coleoptera eating the material when it was sufficiently soft to be ingested. Springtails were also often present in large numbers. Beetles and their larvæ some of which were specific fungus feeders were found tunnelling through the tissues of bracket fungi. These bracket fungi live long enough for the slower growing beetles to complete their life history within their tissues. Mammals also occasionally eat woodland fungi. Badgers will dig for truffles, and on one occasion remains of the Jews Ear fungus (*Hirneola auricula-judae*) were found in the stomach of a dead badger. The smaller fungus-eaters in their turn were eaten by birds, and so to the food chains already described.

Dead plant remains also provide food directly for a host of animals which are mainly very small. Of these, perhaps the springtails and the mites are the most important. These were found to be present in the leaf litter in considerable numbers when examined with the help of a Berlese funnel. They were not distributed in a haphazard manner, but showed preference habitats. For example, in the leaf litter it was the mites that occurred in greatest numbers, while below on the better-decayed humus the springtails were the dominant types. It was estimated for a beech wood that there were up to forty million mites and twenty-eight million springtails per acre, and although no counts were attempted at Thurlbear, the numbers were obviously very great. All these animals feed on decaying plant matter—mainly dead leaves from the plants above. The leaves are first acted upon by bacteria and fungi before their consistence is such that these animals can eat them. It appeared likely that the mites were able to tackle this material at an earlier stage in decay than the springtails. When the humus was incorporated more completely in the top soil, the earthworms had their share. In fact, it is largely due to their activity that decayed leaves are dragged into the soil. In Thurlbear, however, with its clay soil, this was not particularly obvious, the earthworm population being confined largely to the top few inches where the humus content was high and the soil much more crumbly.

The mites and springtails may be eaten directly by small birds rooting amongst the leaf litter, but more particularly they form the food of smaller carnivores. Harvestmen are known to eat both mites and springtails. Ground beetles also eat them and no doubt many other inhabitants of the leaf litter community. These in their turn are eaten by insectivorous birds, and so to the larger carnivores once more.

When animals die they soon become the food of other animals. This is most obvious in the case of mammals and birds which are large enough to support an easily visible population. Within a very short time of death—often within a few hours—flies such as bluebottles (*Calliphora sp.*) lay their eggs on the dead bodies, and at warm temperatures these may hatch within twenty-four hours. The larvæ, although unable to eat solid food, soon reduce the protein to soluble material by enzyme secretion, and quickly transform the flesh into a slimy mass.

The burying beetles are also important scavengers. *Necrophorus humator*, which is a large black beetle, and *Necrophorus vespillo*, which has chestnut bands, were particularly common in Thurlbear. These lay their eggs on the carrion and then proceed to bury it by removing earth from underneath. The larvæ soon hatch out and feed on the flesh.

There are many other species of beetle that are carrion feeders. On a dead stoat found on a path in Thurlbear woods there were specimens of *Onthophagus ovatus*, a small lamellicorn beetle, several very active staphylinids (*Ortholestes murinus*) and six clavicorns (*Thanatophilus rugosus*), besides a number of smaller species—mainly staphylinids. Later, when most of the flesh had gone, beetles belonging to the genus *Dermestes* were found inside the bones, taking the work of destruction a stage further.

Dung also provides food for a large variety of animals. Its composition was found to vary very much from species to species. For example, fox dung consisted largely of animal remains ; the bones and fur of rabbits or the feathers of birds being easily distinguished when the dung was analysed. Badger dung contained both animal and vegetable remains— the latter usually predominating. The chief animal constituents found were wing cases of Dor-beetles (*Geotrupes sp.*), the fur of young rabbits and an occasional caterpillar skin, while vegetable remains included plant fibres and the seeds of edible fruits.

Flies and beetles are again the chief types which feed on dung, some of them feeding exclusively on this material. In woods it is unusual to find the dung of any animals besides foxes, badgers and rabbits, and the dung of the latter attracts very few scavengers as so little food and moisture remains in it after passing through the gut of the rabbit twice.*

Dor-beetles were occasionally found in the vicinity of badger dung, but besides small flies which oviposit on it, beetles such as staphylinids and those of the genus *Aphodius* were the most common.

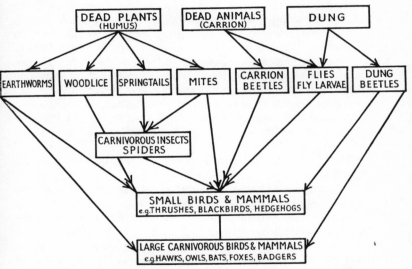

FIG. 14. Food Chains involving Saprophytes and Scavengers.

All these types feeding on carrion and dung are again attacked by birds or mammals and thus lead to the larger carnivores once more.

(3) *Food Chains involving Parasites*

Food chains may become extremely complicated when parasites are taken into account, but in the majority of cases it is not necessary to include them because they are eaten along

* The moist pellets voided at night are eaten once more and water and further food extracted.

with the host by the predator. This is usually true of endoparasites such as tapeworms and nematodes. In fact, in the former case it is the usual means of transference of the bladder-worm stage of the parasite from one host to another.

Parasitoids, however, are in a different category as they often provide food in the adult stage for other predators, and so lead to side branches of the food chain. By parasitoid one means the type of parasite such as an ichneumon which lives in the larval state on a host not much bigger than itself, which it eventually destroys. They are all insects belonging either to the hymenoptera or diptera, and a number of kinds were found in this woodland community. Some of them were discovered by breeding lepidopterous larvæ collected in the wood; these included both tachinid-flies and ichneumons. The adult ichneumons of larger size were often seen flying amongst the vegetation or visiting flower heads ; smaller ones were found by sweeping.

These parasitoids form the food of a number of birds and spiders, and so enter the main food chains.

Parasitic food chains, however, are not always confined to a single parasite, as many have hyperparasites parasitic on them. It is not unusual to find that chalcid wasps have laid their eggs in the ichneumon or tachinid-fly grub which is parasitic on other larvæ. This is only discovered by breeding the host larvæ and seeing what hatches out. Many insect parasites are associated with galls.

If these are collected when the larvæ inside are mature, the parasites as well as the gall formers may emerge in due course. The marble gall is a good one to illustrate this ; they should be collected in September and kept in a jam jar with cloth cover, damping them slightly at intervals. It must, however, be borne in mind that living within these galls there may be species of inquilines. These are not parasites, but guest-flies. They do not cause galls to be formed themselves, but live within the gall tissues. It is not always easy at first to distinguish between hosts, parasites and inquilines when breeding them. The parasites, however, are usually tiny chalcids which can readily be recognized by the almost entire absence of veins in the wings, and often by their metallic blue or green coloured bodies. The inquilines are usually distinguished from gall wasps by their black colour and shorter wings, but there are exceptions.

(4) *Size and Numbers in Relation to Food Chains*

Having studied some of the food chains in woodland, it was obvious that there were certain principles that were true for most of them. The first was the importance of size in determining the position of an animal in its food chain. In a chain of several species those animals which were at the plant end of the chain were smaller than those at the other. Thus the aphids were smaller than the ladybirds or syrphid larvæ, and these in turn were smaller than the sparrowhawks. To take another example, the springtails and mites were smaller than the harvest-spiders, which were smaller than the predaceous ground beetles, which were eaten by the much larger hedgehogs, foxes or badgers.

Exceptions to this principle are to be found in parasitic food chains, where the parasite is smaller than its host, and if hyperparasites are present these are smaller still. This principle of size is intimately connected with that of number. On the whole it is true to say that the small animals are the most numerous, and as you go up the food chain, the numbers become less. On beating an oak bough and counting the types on the beating tray, it became obvious at a glance that the aphids and small bugs were in the majority by a very long way and that there were only a few spiders or ladybirds ; in the wood itself there were a relatively small number of warblers and tits, and only one pair of sparrow hawks.

This principle of numbers results from the fact that small animals in general are able to reproduce at a faster rate than large ones, and therefore provide a far greater number of progeny. This number is far in excess of that needed for replacement in the absence of predators, and hence there is a large surplus for the carnivores to feed upon. As you go further up the food chain the reproductive capacity becomes smaller, and hence the surplus is reduced. This surplus, therefore, can only support a much more limited number of predators, until finally at the end of a food chain reproduction rates are so low that the surplus, if any, is insufficient to support a predator at all. These principles involving size and numbers are conveniently summarized by what has been described by Elton as the pyramid of numbers.

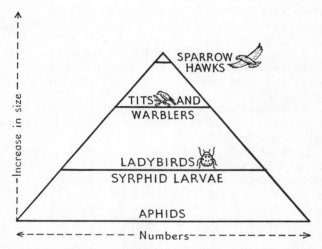

Fig. 15.   Diagram illustrating the Pyramid of Numbers in a Woodland Food Chain.

The fact that parasites are exceptions to this principle is due to the fact that they are living normally on one individual and cannot change hosts when that one is eaten up ; they must, therefore, feed at a pace which does not kill the host, and hence must take only the limited amount of food which the host can then replace. This necessitates a smaller size than that of the host.

PLATE V

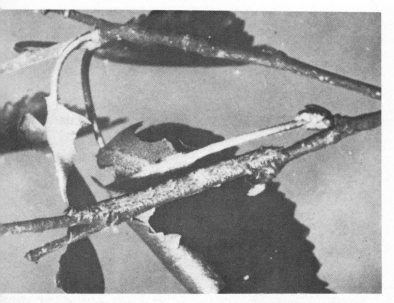

A. Protective Resemblance. Grey Arches Moth at rest on lichened tree-trunk.

B. Protective Resemblance. Light Emerald Moth larva in protective position.

PLATE VI

A. *Right :* Long-eared Bat.

B. *Below :* A Badger emerges as dusk deepens. A nocturnal animal at the end of a food chain.

(5) *Flexibility of Food Chains*

So far we have built up a general picture of inter-relationships based on food chains. The tendency, however, is to produce as a result a concept of rigid connection between one type and another. Although this rigidity is found in some instances, we have to modify these ideas considerably as the majority of food chains are very flexible things, and in reality vary a great deal as the environmental factors alter. Feeding in some types is a more or less continuous process, many insects, for example, in their larval states feed practically all the time except when they are about to moult. In these cases —mainly confined to herbivores—the food chain of which they are a part is a fairly continuous one. In the majority of animals, however, there is a feeding and resting rhythm, often associated with day and night, and this leads to an alteration of the food chains of which they are part.

This change in the food chain is illustrated most obviously in animals which are strictly nocturnal or crepuscular, but it is nevertheless true to some extent for many animals which have preference habits such as foxes, which normally feed at dusk and at night, but which occasionally do so in the daytime.

Night-watching in a wood can be a fascinating and exciting experience. We found it useful to list the sequence of events that took place from dusk onwards ; and this vividly expressed the change in activity. At first all the sights and sounds were typical of day activity. Bird song and movement became restricted, there was a return to the wood of those birds which normally roost there, but which spend the day in the surrounding country: pigeons, magpies, carrion crows, and an occasional cuckoo came into this category. A robin would investigate its territory, obviously aware of our presence, however still we kept. The last bird sounds were those of the blackbird which became more intermittent and shorter as dusk deepened. The period of quiet before the nocturnal types took their place was quite short. The cry of the tawny owl was soon heard, and the whirr of the nightjar a little later.

The mammals showed the same sequence, although less obviously, as few mammals were seen in the day. When watching by a badger set, the first sign was the return of a grey squirrel to its drey where it spent the night. Rabbits emerged from their burrows and nibbled vegetation somewhat tentatively in the vicinity of their homes before leaving the wood for the pasture outside. A fox went silently past soon after, and the first sign of a badger was at late dusk when things were somewhat difficult to distinguish. Bats had appeared earlier to make use of the period when the crepuscular insects were active. When quite dark, wood mice could be heard jumping amongst the leaves, the badgers went off to their feeding grounds, and an occasional hedgehog was heard.

The same applied to the insects. Butterfly activity stopped long before sundown, though the purple hairstreak (*Thecla quercus*) gave an occasional flutter where a patch of sun still struck one part of an oak tree—this, however, only occurred on very warm evenings. As dusk approached the midges and mosquitoes became active—this was their main feeding period. The first moths were mainly geometers, an occasional carpet moth being seen fluttering among the shrubs. Later the noctuids flew by with swifter flight, and an occasional dor-beetle or cockchafer would blunder by.

With the help of a torch it was noticed that on the oak branches there was much more obvious activity than during the day. Caterpillars were actively eating, spiders were searching for prey, while aphids carried on as usual. On damp nights slugs and snails left their hiding places among the leaf litter and were crawling over the vegetation, a few slugs ascending the bigger trees presumably to feed on the epiphytic algæ on the trunks. In the leaf litter earwigs, woodlice and ground beetles were seen in an active state searching for food after a day of relative inactivity.

The whole picture was one of change over from one type of activity to another, one group taking over from another in the general food chains. It was difficult to discover the many details of this change, but some of them were fairly obvious.

Worms in the pasture land outside the wood mainly eaten by moles during the day, became the food of badgers on wet nights as they lay on the surface. As many as forty worms were found in one badger's stomach on one occasion.

The butterflies which were occasionally eaten by birds during the day were replaced by the moths at night, which were fed upon by bats, nightjars, and to a slight extent by owls. Tawny owls were also found to eat bats on occasion, as proved by pellet analysis. Other crepuscular and nocturnal insects like mosquitoes, dor-beetles and cockchafers were preyed upon by the same types, and the last two also by badgers and occasionally foxes. The voles which formed the prey of weasels during the day, were replaced by the wood mice which were eaten by tawny owls and badgers at night. The smaller members of the leaf litter community were eaten by the carabid beetles which in turn became the food of the hedgehogs and badgers as they routed amongst the leaves. Although the picture was so incomplete, the general principle was clear that the diurnal food chains were not necessarily the same as the nocturnal ones ; usually they were quite different, due to the contrasting habits of the animals ; sometimes they overlapped, especially when the organisms were less strict in their time rhythm.

These rhythmic changes in the food chains, however, were not confined to twenty-four hours, but also occurred more gradually over the year. The most obvious of these was the change from summer to winter, with autumn and spring as the transition periods. Although these changes were obvious, the reasons for them are complex and by no means easy to unravel, although certain environmental factors obviously play their part.

The most important of these are the drop in temperature and the reduction in day length and light intensity, although wind and rainfall fluctuation also play a part. The climate of this country is such that the change-over from summer to winter results in a sufficient drop in temperature to reduce the metabolism of most cold-blooded woodland types to a level where normal activity is impossible. This applies particularly to insects and molluscs. These animals pass the winter in various ways. Many of them hibernate, slugs and snails being found buried in the soil and under the loose bark of logs. Insects were always difficult to find as they were invariably hidden from their potential predators. Some passed the winter as adults, but the majority in the egg, larval or pupal stages. Aphids, for example, wintered as eggs, the larger ones being seen quite easily on careful inspection of the twigs. Larval stages of some insects such as beetles and noctuids were found in the soil among the more superficial roots of the plants, and pupæ, especially of moths, were found at the bases of tree trunks under the moss and between projecting roots. Adult insects especially beetles were found amongst the leaf litter and under the bark of fallen trees. The overall picture was of a tremendous reduction in the number of insects, those that were present being extremely well hidden and in the main inactive.

This result was not due entirely to temperature although it appeared to be the main factor. Most of these types were vegetarians, and leaf fall brought on by changes in day length and to some extent temperature, robbed them of food.

We divided up the birds found at Thurlbear into residents, summer migrants and winter migrants, and found out as much as possible about their feeding habits, and from the literature available. Some interesting points emerged. It soon became evident that the summer migrants which were mainly insectivorous were fairly strict in their feeding habits. This applied to the various warblers—wood, willow and chiff-chaff—which confined themselves very largely to insects, and to a slightly less extent to the nightingale. The nightjar, also, was almost exclusively an insect eater. The residents fell into two groups. Those such as woodpeckers and treecreepers which had special adaptations and could find insect and other invertebrate food; and those which were more adaptable and could utilize a much wider range of food. Thus the tits, wren and robin, although mainly insectivorous, made quite extensive use of seeds during the winter. The blackbird was found to be especially adaptable, feeding on a great variety of food found in woods.

Scarcity of food may result in difficult times for mammals. They may migrate southwards as from the more northern regions of the world. Or some may hibernate or partially hibernate. The dormouse hibernates, but no specimens were seen at Thurlbear. Bats and hedgehogs were present, and they partially hibernated. The larger mammals such as the fox which do not hibernate must presumably work harder to get enough food. But the badger, being more omnivorous, relied more on vegetable food during autumn and winter. Fruit, berries, grass, and other green vegetation figured largely in its diet during the colder months, but in spring and summer its diet consisted mainly or wholly of animal food which at such times was easily obtainable.

Thus winter, with its resulting migrations, hibernation and reductions in numbers, causes much change in the summer food chains. Some continued as before, but the majority were modified or were absent altogether.

Food chains may also be affected by climatic changes other than those which are regular and seasonal. Exceptionally cold winters undoubtedly have an important selective effect on the types of organisms which survive, and on their numbers. Although no work on this aspect of the subject was attempted at Thurlbear, it was quite obvious from year to year that there were great fluctuations in the numbers of certain species or groups, and these would undoubtedly have an effect on the more normal food chains, taxing the adaptability of the various species to varying extents. As a generalization it can be said that these periodic extremes of climatic conditions tend to eliminate those species that are at the edge of their range, and which are thus less perfectly adapted to this particular habitat.

CHAPTER IX

COMPETITION AND FEEDING ADAPTATIONS

BEFORE we leave the subject of food relationships it would be useful to bring some of the principles together to broaden the concept of the woodland community. So far we have largely confined ourselves to main groups of feeders, vegetarians, carnivores, scavengers and so on. We then divided them up into smaller categories according to their specialized modes of feeding such as defoliators, leaf-miners, root-feeders, wood-borers and many others. This latter was useful in showing how the whole economy of the wood was utilized by some group or other, and no potential food supply was left untouched. We also saw that there was a very definite relationship between one organism and another through food chains and the food cycle. These relationships, however, were not as rigid as appeared at first sight, as there was much adaptability according to the changing conditions within the wood, either daily, seasonal, or as a result of climatic action.

The whole concept of inter-relationships was broadened, however, when we considered the important aspect of competition for food. This competition could be inter-specific, or between individuals of the same species. Inter-specific competition for food undoubtedly occurs throughout the whole community and leads in the more obvious cases to the biological niche to which we have already referred. This concept, however, can be taken a step further if we consider a single group of related animals where the number of species present in the wood is small, such as birds and mammals.

D. K. Colquhoun has shown * how woodland birds are beautifully adapted to cover the food available. Each species has its own particular feeding habits, made possible by structural adaptation. This results in a parcelling out of

* Colquhoun, M. K., and Morley, A. (see Bibliography).

COMPETITION AND FEEDING ADAPTATIONS   75

the available food so that there is enough for each without much overlap. This minimizes inter-specific struggle and is an important adaptation for survival, especially in winter when conditions are difficult and food comparatively scarce.

Thus the greater spotted woodpecker with its pincer-like toes and stout tail acting as a prop, is able to cling to the sides of trees, and with its strong pointed bill quickly probe the tough wood to get to the wood-boring and bark-eating organisms which form its food. The tree creeper, on the other hand, is a nimble bird which feeds largely on the types which hide in the crevices of the bark. To find enough food it has to cover great areas of this specialized habitat, and thus methodically works each tree trunk in turn in a series of rapid spirals from the base, pausing at intervals to extract some insect or spider with its fine slightly-curved beak.

The smaller branches, twigs and leaves are the hunting grounds of other insectivorous birds, but again the distribution is not haphazard although there is inevitably some overlap. In winter, when observation was easier, we studied the feeding habits of the various birds in Thurlbear, and were able to confirm, by counting the number of each species according to feeding level, the fact that Colquhoun had brought out that most species had preference feeding areas. Thus the blue-tits and long-tailed tits fed largely in the upper layers on the smaller twigs, the great tit preferred the shrubs and the small boughs, while the wren largely fed in the herb layer or the lower parts of the shrubs.

The blackbird and robin, during the winter at any rate, fed largely on leaf-litter fauna. Scarcity of food, however, led to adaptation of feeding behaviour, and in cold wintry weather it was not unusual to find flocks of tits leaving their preference levels and searching amongst the leaf litter where food was more abundant. Thus there appeared to be a type of un-conscious co-operation amongst the various species of birds, by which best use was made of the available food and the essential structure of the community was kept intact.

TABLE VII

TABLE TO ILLUSTRATE PREFERENCE FEEDING HABITATS OF WOODLAND BIRDS

(Summary of three counts taken during December)

NAME	TREE CANOPY	SHRUBS	GROUND
Long-tailed Tit . .	26	1	0
Coal Tit . . .	2	0	0
Blue Tit . . .	19	2	2
Great Tit . . .	3	0	3
Robin . . .	0	6	6
Pigeon . . .	27	0	0
Wren . . .	0	7	0
Blackbird . . .	0	1	4
Pheasant . . .	0	0	1
Woodcock . . .	0	0	2
Greater Spotted Wood-pecker.	1 (on boughs)	0	0
Tree Creeper . .	1 (on trunk)	0	0

Competition between members of the same species for food is a potential danger which may have serious effects, but under normal circumstances it seldom arises. Thus the majority of insects lay their eggs in numbers which are not large enough to cause difficulties when the larvæ hatch. This is particularly true of some of the smaller woodland organisms —especially the vegetarians, but when you come to the larger carnivores you have types which are feeding on a smaller surplus population, and it may be that a wide range of country has to be searched before adequate food is found. Mammals and birds protect themselves from the difficulty of competition from this cause by having territories.

The possession of a territory is not necessarily merely a device for ensuring adequate dispersal in terms of food supply, but is best looked upon as an adaptation to a complex of factors of which food supply is usually the most important.

The larger carnivorous mammals such as badgers and foxes show strong territorial instincts, the territories often being very large. Over the whole of the Thurlbear wood area there was only one occupied badger set in which a pair of badgers normally lived. This set consisted of six holes and was not occupied all the year round but appeared to be an alternative residence to a larger set situated about a mile away where activity was more constant. This is characteristic of the species, and their territory would appear to comprise a large area of country with these two sets more or less in the centre. From studies conducted in various other parts it seems likely that these badger territories usually consist of some four or five square miles of mixed country, but they are smaller where food is abundant and the population density is high. In the vicinity of the sets the territory is well marked, but towards the extremities the feeding areas overlap with those of their neighbours. The marking out of the territory is almost certainly done by setting scent, the secretion from their musk glands being very potent. This takes place on paths, vegetation and the base of trees or shrubs. The number of badgers occupying the territory varies from one to three pairs, the number varying according to the age of the set and the food available in the vicinity. When the numbers reach maximum density the cubs leave the district and form territories of their own elsewhere or take the place of other badgers which have died.

Badgers are creatures of habit and it is easy to find and map out the network of paths which radiate from the sets. It follows that the paths which are best defined are those most used, and therefore more important in the badger's life. These are found to be the ones which join up one set with another and which lead to the main feeding areas. This was done for the set in Thurlbear wood although in this instance, being a small set, and not used all the year, not all the characteristics of a larger community were present.

Foxes also show territorial behaviour, though we found it most difficult to study. As far as could be ascertained only

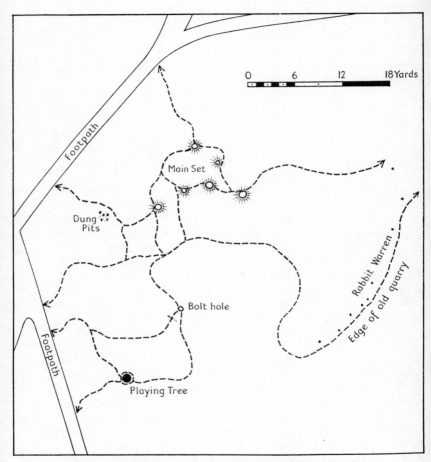

FIG. 16. Map of a small Badger Set in Thurlbear Wood.
---------- Badger paths.

one pair inhabited the wood at the breeding season, the dog fox leading a much less restricted life than the vixen during the breeding season. Thus it seems probable that the same general principles apply to both fox and badger, the territory being a wide area centring about two or three alternative earths of which one is used for breeding. In this case the breeding earth was a disused badger set.

Little is known as to how territories in badgers and foxes are maintained. That there is an instinctive " respect " for another's territory is fairly certain, as defence of the territory is not a conspicuous feature. Trespassing, however, does occur and is usually tolerated except near the breeding centre, and there only at certain times. For instance, roaming badgers are usually free to wander anywhere except when the cubs are small, and possibly in the late autumn when food is becoming more scarce and optimum density becomes an important factor. In the fox it is the period between mating and the dispersal of the cubs when the visitors are unwelcome. Fights do occur on occasions, more often with foxes than badgers, but at least one instance of the latter has been recorded. It is also probable that badger cubs when nearly fully grown are forcibly ejected from the parental set in October.

Much work has been done on bird territories, and much more is known about it than is the case for mammals. For the majority of woodland birds territory is confined to the spring and summer, but there are exceptions. Robins at Thurlbear were found fairly evenly distributed over the area ; they had both summer and winter territories. The same appeared to apply to the buzzards, sparrow hawks and greater spotted woodpeckers. Only one pair of each of these species was found in the area. The wood itself probably defined the territory of the woodpecker, but the buzzards and sparrow hawks included quite a large area outside the wood in addition.

Summer territories were most marked among the smaller insectivorous birds such as the various species of warblers and the nightingale. Singing trees or bushes were quite obvious for these species in April, and it was surprising how many there were in the area, especially chiff-chaffs, willow-warblers and nightingales. It was not easy to define their territories exactly except along the outer edges of the wood where they were most often seen or heard. With insect food so abundant in the spring it would appear to be immaterial at first sight to have territory, as competition between members of the same species for food could not have serious results. It has been pointed out, however, that it is not just sufficiency of food that is important. If very cold weather should coincide with the first few days after the hatching of the young birds, the nest must not be left for long or else the young will quickly die of exposure. Food must, therefore, be found in sufficient quantity in a very short time so there must be an abundance of it. This, of course, does not apply to those species where cock and hen incubate in turn, but it may be an important factor for some species.

As is well known, birds defend their territory by aggressive display and song, facts which were easily confirmed by observation in the spring.

These aspects of feeding habits force us to modify the usual understanding of the phrase " struggle for existence " which is often misleadingly simplified into a conception of " Nature red in tooth and claw." Inter-relationships can only be understood when we take into account the various aspects of the struggle for life including " co-operation " between the members of a community—an important aspect often ignored.

CHAPTER X

PROTECTIVE ADAPTATIONS

WE have referred to the fact that animals have three main purposes in life—seeking food, self-preservation and reproducing their kind. So far we have confined ourselves to those adaptations which are largely concerned with feeding. Now let us consider some of the adaptations of woodland animals to their second main purpose—self-preservation.

One of the most striking things about woodland in the daytime is the comparatively small number of animals you see. There may be a few birds busy amongst the tree tops or routing amongst the leaf litter, a few butterflies mainly in the sunnier patches or along the paths, and a larger number of diptera or hymenoptera, once more in the sunny parts. The majority of organisms, although in reality so abundant, are hidden from the casual observer and have to be searched for by various means before being discovered. This is due to the wonderful and varied ways in which they are protectively adapted. Some of these adaptations are structural, others concern the behaviour of the animal.

H. B. Cott, in his admirable book *Adaptive Coloration in Animals*, has brought out the underlying principles. Observation at Thurlbear provided many instances of protective devices.

Among the small herbivorous insects, general colour resemblance to the food plant was the usual rule. Thus the majority of leaf feeders such as aphids and various caterpillars were green. This was correlated with their behaviour. Being small, with an abundance of food present in the immediate vicinity, little movement was necessary, so the generalized green colour remained a useful camouflage. It is only when an animal is active and still uniform in colour that movement from one microhabitat to another may render it conspicuous by having to pass across a different coloured background. This difficulty was avoided by some of the larger larvæ by

their behaviour ; they remained motionless during the day
and became active at night.

A generalized mottling is a more useful camouflage for types
which habitually rest on tree-trunks or the ground. This was
very evident in the case of many moths, whose fore-wings
resembled the bark of trees, such as the copper underwing
(*Amphipyra pyramidea*), or the lichens that covered them,
such as the pale brindled beauty (*Phigalia pilosaria*). It
was also true of those which spent the day hiding amongst
the leaf litter and ground vegetation, such as the large yellow
underwing (*Triphaena pronuba*).

This type of camouflage was again correlated with behaviour,
such as their immobility during the day, and the manner in
which they folded their wings to render the otherwise conspicuous hind wings invisible. Specimens of the old lady
moth (*Mormo maura*) orientated their position on the tree
trunk so that the dark markings on their wings coincided
with, or ran in a similar direction to, the cracks in the bark.

This generalized mottling was also evident to a marked
degree in ground nesting or ground resting birds met with in
Thurlbear. The hen pheasant was an excellent example of
the former and the woodcock of the latter. As far as was
known, the woodcock did not nest there, but it was a regular
winter visitor.

Insects, whose main predators are birds, are recognized
largely by shape and colour ; and a common device amongst
woodland animals is to have their outline broken up so that
their shape appears to be different. This may delay recogni-
tion, even if it does not prevent it altogether. Examples of
this disruptive coloration were noticed on several occasions.
Some of the carpet moths, such as the silver-ground carpet
(*Xanthorhoë montanata*) when at rest would have been quite
conspicuous if it were not for the prominent black band on
each wing which broke up the typical moth shape. The
caterpillar of the comma butterfly (*Polygonia c-album*) with
its conspicuous white patch appeared to be broken up into
smaller pieces and so no longer resembled a larva.

The shape of an animal is made more conspicuous by its bulk, its thickness throwing the shape into relief. Various devices were found in animals which reduce this danger, such as the elimination of shadow and counter-shading. Moths when at rest on tree trunks spread their wings flat so that shadow was removed. Caterpillars were also found which had devices for eliminating the shadow that, due to their roundness, would render them more conspicuous. One of the most striking of these was that of the light emerald moth (*Metrocampa margaritaria*) which in the daytime remained flat against a twig along its whole length, getting rid of the shadow between the twig and itself by a fringe of hairs on either side which bridged the gap. This made it look like a thickening of the stem on which it was lying. These caterpillars were only discovered by beating.

In larger animals the appearance of flatness is often produced by countershading. In rabbits, as for most mammals, the underparts are lighter than the upper, and there is a gradation of colouring between the two. As a light surface reflects more light to the eyes than a darker one, this evens out the intensity of the reflected rays from both surfaces, and produces an appearance of flatness. The result, in the dusk especially, as the rabbits emerged from their holes, was most effective. The same applied to the wood mice and voles, and to a lesser extent to the fox and stoat.

Some of the most effective cases of camouflage were those which resembled specific objects in the environment. Caterpillars of the purple hairstreak butterfly (*Thecla quercus*) with their patches of brown colour and their positional behaviour, exactly resembled the scales on the oak buds. Resemblance to twigs was also a common feature in moth larvæ, the most striking being those of the oak beauty (*Pachys strataria*) and the various species of thorn moths (*Ennomos sp.*). These by their rigid behaviour during the day and their extraordinary bumps, rings and other markings, were almost impossible to detect in their natural habitat. All were found by beating rather than searching. Another beautiful example of resemblance to specific objects found in the wood was the beetle *Cionus scrophulariae*. This weevil was found on figwort plants. When the larvæ were ready to pupate, they formed cocoons amongst the developing figwort capsules which they resembled to an amazing extent. When the adults hatched out, they sat about on the young buds and were again extremely difficult to detect. As if that were not enough, on being touched they would draw up their legs, tuck in their snout, and drop to the ground, where they looked just like larval droppings.

The comma butterfly with its dark colouring on the underside and its scalloped wings, looked amazingly like a dead oak leaf, and whether it was among green ones when at rest, or brown ones during hibernation, it was extremely difficult to detect.

Mimetic types were also found which, by resembling other insects that were poisonous or bad-tasting, were able to claim some degree of immunity from attack. Thus a number of syrphid flies resembled bees and wasps, and species of clear-wing moths various species of hymenoptera. The wasp beetle (*Clytus arietis*) like so many of the better mimetic types, in addition to resembling in a general way the black and yellow coloration of the wasp, showed by its behaviour a similar remarkable likeness. Thus one specimen that was observed was hovering tentatively round the base of a tree, and after alighting ran swiftly about its surface in the exact manner often noted in wasps of the genus *Vespa*. Mimetic behaviour in addition to colour similarities were also noted in the narrow bordered bee hawk moth (*Hemaris tityus*) whose larvæ fed on the Devil's bit scabious (*Scabiosa succisa*) which bordered the paths. These moths mimicked bumble bees by their flight, and in their habit of flying in sunshine and visiting similar flowers such as the bugle.

Warning coloration was not a very notable means of protection employed by woodland creatures, although a few instances were noted such as wasps with their characteristic yellow and black colour. The black-and-white

PLATE VII

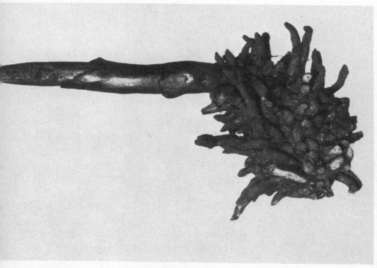

A. Lichens on an oak bough. These provide food and shelter for many small insects.

B. Bird's nest orchid, showing adventitious root system.

PLATE VIII

Thurlbear Wood from the south-west, showing colonisation of rough grazing in the foreground and the formation of scrub near the wood.

face of the badger was also found to be a good example of the
best type of warning coloration for nocturnal animals.
Other woodland animals use protective coverings to effect
concealment. Some of the most interesting of these were the
larvæ of lacewings which, when beaten from the oaks in the
spring, were extremely difficult to see on the beating tray
until they moved, due to the assortment of debris which they
carried over their body in the manner of a caddis. Frog-
hopper nymphs in their frothy covering or cuckoo-spit also
derive protection in this way, though it is probable that the
covering also serves to prevent desiccation, the cuticle of the
nymph being unusually thin.

The larvæ of certain moths have the habit of rolling the
leaves and feeding inside, getting protection to some extent
from the habitat. The commonest of these found was the
green oak-roller moth (*Tortrix viridiana*) which was so
abundant during one May that the noise of their droppings
falling from the oaks on to the hazels below was continuous.
These, incidentally, were the chief defoliators of oak found in
the wood, although the larvæ of the mottled umber moth
(*Erannis defoliaria*) were abundant on occasions.

Some of the more active woodland creatures used their
powers of movement as their chief method of avoiding their
enemies. This was particularly true of adult insects which
were able to escape by flight. The slow but erratic flight of
the speckled wood butterfly (*Pararge aegeria*) in a woodland
glade, coupled with its mottled colouring, made it very
difficult to follow as it passed through patches of sunshine
and shadow. The conspicuousness of the majority of butterflies when in flight is probably an indication of the effectiveness
of flight alone as a means of escape.

Birds, of course, also use flight as the chief means of escape
from enemies. This is often coupled with the ability to fly to
dense cover when followed by larger bird predators such as
the sparrow-hawk.

Many animals rely to some extent on speed of running,
ground beetles, staphylinid beetles and centipedes among the

leaf litter provided good examples of this among smaller animals, but many mammals rely on this method too, especially the smaller herbivores like the wood mouse and the bank vole. The former especially is an extremely agile creature moving in a series of leaps and runs, compared with the straight run of the house mouse. This ability to jump is a specialized adaptation for avoiding enemies that is very effective and was to be found in many groups of animals. The springtails in the leaf litter when disturbed jumped about in all directions and were very difficult to capture. Beetles showed a similar ability, especially members of the genus *Chalcoides*. Two species of these tiny metallic beetles with greatly thickened femora for jumping were found on the sallows growing in the wetter parts of the wood. Squirrels used the same method of escaping enemies, and with their aerial jumps and ability to use cover, hiding behind the far side of the tree, they easily avoided capture.

Other woodland types were able to get away from their enemies by building some retreat into which they could go when danger threatened. This was true of the majority of the woodland mammals. Rabbits bolted for their holes when danger threatened, thumping hard with their hind limbs if there was time to warn others. Foxes and badgers had their underground homes, the latter in some districts building almost impregnable fortresses which are used for countless generations, each new tenant adding to the complexity of the system of tunnels and chambers underground. At Thurlbear the set was fairly recent and appeared to be a smaller system than usual.

Wood mice, voles and stoats also used underground tunnels, while squirrels sometimes made use of hollow trees, as did the bats. Sometimes these retreats acted as bolt holes, but in addition they were useful during times of inactivity. In mammals this was usually the daytime when activity would often have made them conspicuous.

Some woodland birds used the same method for times when they were inactive or helpless. Many of them such as the greater spotted woodpecker, nuthatch and the various tits, rested in tree holes. In fact, it has been shown that the optimum density of many species such as the tits is governed by the number of suitable tree holes for nesting purposes. Experiments done in the Forest of Dean * showed that by providing a large number of nest boxes, the breeding tit population was considerably increased.

The examples cited in this section form just a small selection of the many and varied adaptations which aid self-preservation, but they are enough to show how important these adaptations are in the life of a woodland community.

* Mackenzie, J. M. D.

CHAPTER XI

ADAPTATIONS RELATING TO REPRODUCTION AND LIFE HISTORY

THE types of animal reproduction met with in any community are numerous and tend to follow similar principles in most habitats. We therefore confined our attention to cases of adaptation which were particularly connected with woodland ; only a few of these will be mentioned here.

Specialized methods of egg laying were noted which were adapted to woodland conditions. Many of these involved the use of the woody portions of the trees. Some of the hymenoptera, for example, had specially modified ovipositors for inserting the eggs. One of the larger ichneumons was seen drilling into a decayed trunk with its $\frac{3}{4}$-inch ovipositor, doubtless in search of a hidden wood-boring larva. The species of ichneumon was not identified, but its actions were very similar to those described for *Rhyssa persuasoria*. It ran rapidly over the trunk, with antennæ repeatedly touching the wood. It reared up its body as it inserted its ovipositor, and the series of drill-like motions were seen as it probed deeper and deeper. At intervals it withdrew the instrument, perhaps to remove the sawdust as a man with a drill.

Many of the bark and wood-boring beetles have specialized methods of ovipositing. The oak bark beetle (*Scolytus intricatus*) was common, and the galleries made by the adults and larvæ were easily seen on stripping the bark. The female makes a wider horizontal gallery and lays the eggs in special niches made at intervals in it. When the larvæ hatch they make much smaller tunnels which radiate outwards from the main one forming a characteristic pattern.

The eggs of some wood-borers are laid in cracks of the bark and the larvæ on hatching are able to penetrate the wood by means of their strong mandibles. The longhorn beetle

(*Rhagium inquisitor*) was found commonly in rotting oak wood and was a good example of this type.

The nut weevils (*Balaninus spp.*) had very specialized methods of ovipositing. Two species were commonly found by beating in the early summer, *B. nucum* and *B. venosus*. These lay their eggs in the developing acorns or hazel nuts. They do this by drilling a hole with their abnormally long rostrum which has a pair of strong mandibles at the end, and then depositing the eggs in the tunnel thus made. The larvæ feed on the growing nut and emerge in the autumn and pupate in the soil. The exit hole in the shell was a conspicuous feature of many a fallen hazel nut.

As was mentioned previously, many of the woodland birds nested in tree holes, the woodpecker using its strong bill to excavate its tunnel, while the tits and owls made use of holes already made. A treecreeper on the other hand made use of a piece of loose bark to nest behind. Nuthatches also nested in holes, plastering up the entrance of a ready-made hole with mud to make it the right size.

Some specimens of sawflies have interesting methods of egg laying. Some have a saw-like ovipositor which is used to slit up the edge of a leaf before laying the eggs in the pocket thus formed.

Other reproductive adaptations concern the methods by which woodland animals find their mates. It is usually very difficult to assess by observation alone what factors are of greatest significance for this, but some idea can be gained in certain instances.

Scent is obviously of great importance in many insects. Work done on assembling in moths has shown how males are attracted to a female when her scent glands are active. This was particularly obvious in the case of the winter moth (*Operophtera brumata*) where the female is wingless. Females hatched out in late November from larvæ beaten from the oaks, when taken to the wood quickly attracted the winged males on mild nights.

It is probable, too, that scent plays an important part in

the mating behaviour of mammals. In badgers, for example, it seems to be certain that setting scent at various points on the territory by a female wanting a mate is the main means of attracting a wandering male. In this connection it is of interest to note that it is the females which tend to remain in the parental sets if there is room, and the males that wander.

Vocal sounds are also used largely by some animals for attracting mates. The call of the vixen will attract males from over a wide expanse of country at the mating season, and the same is probably true of other mammals. It is, however, perhaps the birds that use this method more than any other. The bird song, besides being a means of defending and defining territory is also a method by which cock birds attract the hens. This is particularly true of the summer migrants where the males usually arrive first and stake out their territorial claims, and the hens come slightly later.

CHAPTER XII

DISPERSAL ADAPTATIONS

DISPERSAL is essential to reduce competition between individuals of the same species, and to increase the range of the species. Earlier in this account we showed how the flora of the wood showed many specialized ways of dispersal. This was made necessary by the absence of locomotion in plants. With animals the problem is different as most of them have good powers of locomotion, and dispersal is automatically carried out.

Any type of movement, whatever its immediate purpose, may therefore lead to dispersal. Various methods were noted for woodland animals. Some types, especially the tiny herbivores, multiply extremely rapidly, and if their food is abundant it does not matter very much in which direction they move, some at any rate will find sufficient Aphids are good examples of this type, the direction of dispersal being largely dependent upon wind. The same applied to some species of spiders, the long threads of gossamer on which the young ones were borne by the wind being conspicuous in the autumn.

Larger insects with stronger wings use their sense organs to guide them during dispersal flights. These are often olfactory, and presumably help in some cases to keep a species within the boundary of the wood and hence within range of its food plant. If, however, they fly farther, they will be able to scent the vegetation on which they lay eggs and be guided to it by chemotactic responses. Thus for non-migratory types which are specific to woodland habitats one visualizes a sort of pull which keeps them to their particular habitat, but occasionally a few move off for various reasons and may help to colonize new habitats. At Thurlbear, for example, we only saw one specimen of the white admiral butterfly

(*Limenitis camilla*) over several years. It is known that it is extending its range, and breeding colonies exist within twenty miles of the wood, but it has not yet become established at Thurlbear although honeysuckle and oaks abound.

One gets a better conception of the dynamic nature of the woodland community as far as it concerns the non-migrating types by using the analogy of a dish of water. This water consists of moving molecules which are normally kept within the main body of the water by inter-molecular attraction, but occasionally some force will be sufficient to make them break through the surface, and no longer being bound by the attraction of the whole, will wander off, perhaps to unite elsewhere with other similar molecules to form other bodies of water. One can take the analogy further by saying that this dispersal from the community may be caused by both external and internal factors. Excessive wind, for example, may cause evaporation to occur more quickly, and may similarly aid in dispersal of flying insects with insufficient power of flight to regain the wood. Internal factors may also be important, and excessive reproduction leading to over-crowding and hence scarcity of food may lead to a mass movement—a boiling over,* as it were, of the water and a consequent enormous increase in the number of water vapour molecules.

Accidental dispersal probably plays an important part in animal distribution, although how important it is, is difficult to assess. By accidental, one means such movements as being carried in mud, on the feet of birds, in the fur of mammals, or among the feathers of birds.

Some of the most spectacular movements are the migration to and from other parts of the world. These vast movements, concerned largely with reproduction, have been alluded to elsewhere insofar as they affected this community.

Many animal movements are concerned with the finding of food, the direction and distance covered varying according to

* One must not press the analogy too far as boiling over of water is not the result of an increase in the number of molecules, while dispersal in animals is usually the result of reproduction.

its distribution and availability. Some slugs, for example, regularly ascended the tree trunks to browse on the algæ each evening, and had returned to their hiding places by morning. Badgers also were extremely regular in emerging from their sets to go off to different feeding grounds according to season and weather, returning as a rule before dawn.

CHAPTER XIII

NUMBERS

WE have seen how a woodland community consists of a vast number of inter-related species of animals and plants, and that these organisms show considerable variation and adaptation in the manner in which they interact with one another. One important aspect of this variation is the fluctuation in numbers of the various species comprising the food cycle.

Woodland is not a static community ; there is a constant shifting of balance between one species and another according to the fluctuation in their numbers. If you are to try to discover the reasons for these fluctuations, the ecologist sooner or later must come up against the problem of estimating numbers. This is often extremely difficult to do with any accuracy, and the techniques employed leave much to be desired. It is not within the scope of this booklet to do more than indicate some of the methods so we will confine ourselves to a few selected examples of which we have practical experience.

In the section on methods of finding woodland animals several techniques were described which can be adapted for numerical work. The numbers of the larger species in leaf litter, for example, were estimated by taking samples from square metres of the soil surface and sieving on to a white sheet. The average of a number of samples was taken and the population of a larger area calculated from that.

For minute animals like springtails the task is much greater, but with the help of a Berlese funnel it can be done with patience, though results are probably rather wide of the truth.

Worm counts were made by pouring permanganate solution on square sectors of soil surface chosen at random, and the worms that wriggled to the surface were counted.

No accurate method was found for counting the number of

species found on oak or similar trees, though the beating of a single bough on a windless day with a subsequent count, gave some idea of the numbers of the smaller animals. The difficulty was defining the unit. The only method adopted was to count the number of leaves on the small bough which was beaten and relating them to that. The method is, however, open to much criticism when comparison of numbers is made.

Some indication of the number of small mammals was gained by trapping extensively a limited area using baited Longworth traps already described. For larger animals like foxes and badgers direct observation at dusk, made simultaneously on several occasions in the vicinity of the earth or sets in the area proved to be the best method.

It is useful at this point to mention certain theoretical aspects concerned with numbers, although accurate practical results are difficult to obtain.

Each species in a wood appears to have an optimum density at any one time, the number varying according to the changing circumstances of the environment. Above this number the effects of over-crowding become evident, and below it the disadvantages of smaller numbers become apparent.

There are many factors which influence numbers, of which the chief is probably the position of the animal in the general food cycle of the wood. In other words, its enemies largely determine its numbers.

The food supply may also be an important limiting factor in some cases. This is true when man by selective felling reduces the food plant of a species, or when rodents modify the ground flora to an important extent, so affecting the numbers of some of the herbivores dependent on it. We have already seen how food supply is an important factor in promoting territorial behaviour in birds and mammals, thus limiting numbers in a given area.

Man can influence numbers considerably by destroying members of certain species. This may be of great importance in some cases, especially if the animal is at the end of a food chain, such as the fox or sparrow-hawk. In the examples mentioned, this normally results in an increase in the numbers of ground-nesting birds like pheasants in the wood.

Climatic conditions of an extreme type cause great variation in numbers, especially in the less adaptable species, and this has its effect on others. It was shown, for example, by J. M. D. Mackenzie in the Forest of Dean that in 1947 after a hard winter the resident tits using bird boxes fell from fifty-four to twenty, while the numbers of flycatchers, which were migrants and therefore unaffected, rose from thirty-nine to fifty-four—presumably taking advantage of vacant nesting sites.

Parasites, especially parasitoids, may play an important part in regulating numbers ; this is especially true of insects where various types of hymenoptera exert a considerable influence. It was calculated from a large number of larvæ of the marsh fritillary butterfly collected after they had dispersed from their winter hibernaculum that over 90 per cent. contained parasitoids. Many of the lepidopterous larvæ collected from the oaks were also found to be infected in this way. This gives some indication of their importance in regulating numbers.

Epidemics and disease also play their part. It is thought that in the case of some of the smaller rodents which periodically increase in numbers, that the overcrowding leads to a great increase in activity and stress of living, and that eventually this results in exhaustion and the death of the animal. Epidemics are also important in reducing rodent numbers.

These are some of the factors that the ecologist has to bear in mind when studying the reasons for fluctuating numbers in a wood. They help to broaden the concept of the dynamic nature of the community and at the same time emphasize how each species owes its position to a delicate balance between itself and the whole complex of factors in its environment.

CHAPTER XIV

PLANT SUCCESSION

In previous chapters we showed how plants and animals had special adaptations for dispersal by which the range of the various species could be extended if conditions were favourable. We also referred to the fact that woodland was the natural climax vegetation of most of southern England, and that if this area was left alone by man and his domestic animals for a long period it would revert to woodland once more. This involves a series of changes known as succession. Man, in fact, is constantly having to fight against this tendency to revert to woodland in order to keep his pasture suitable for grazing.

Thurlbear wood is bordered on the east by rough pasture which has for many years been regularly grazed by cattle. Before the advent of myxomatosis it was also heavily cropped by rabbits which came from the shelter of the wood each evening to feed. Numbers of dried rabbit pellets on the ant hills scattered over the area suggested that the rabbit population at that time was quite high.

To the south-west of the wood there was a further area of calcareous pasture, which although very similar in soil composition, differed considerably in flora due almost certainly to the fact that it had not been grazed by cattle for a number of years. It was a smaller slightly sloping region which was already showing obvious signs of reverting to woodland. Rabbits were also present in this area, but their numbers appeared to be rather fewer judging by the number of droppings.

The only really satisfactory method of studying succession is to isolate one or more small areas from the main region, and by means of permanent quadrats to study the changes in the flora over a large number of years. To do this it would be necessary to wire off these areas to prevent the access of grazing animals. This was not a practicable proposition for us so we had to be content with a short-term study to see if the main stages in succession could be deduced by studying the present condition of the flora.

It was decided first of all to study in detail the area south-west of B, as this was typical scrub with numerous bushes scattered about in a haphazard manner over the area. The plant species were identified and listed and their distribution noted. It was to be expected that if this area was in fact reverting to woodland we should find that the main flora would be typical of calcareous grassland; this would represent the original flora, but in addition we should find some woodland species appearing which had become established.

On listing the flora we found that in the open areas between the bushes the majority of herbaceous plants were undoubtedly typical of calcareous grassland. These included such grasses as quaking grass (*Briza media*) and heath false brome (*Brachypodium pinnatum*). Pyramid orchids (*Anacamptis pyramidalis*) and bee orchids (*Ophrys apifera*) were present, and a number of Compositae such as mouse-ear hawkweed (*Hieraceum pilosella*), rough hawksbeard (*Crepis biennis*), and lesser knapweed (*Centaurea nigra*). Cathartic flax (*Linum catharticum*), rock rose (*Helianthemum chamaecistus*) and milk-wort (*Polygala vulgaris*) were found commonly, and both yellow-wort (*Blackstonia perfoliata*) and centaury (*Centaurium minus*) were present. Earlier in the year violets (*Viola riviniana*) and wild strawberry (*Fragaria vesca*) were conspicuous, and salad burnet (*Poterium sanguisorba*) was abundant. A more complete list is given to show that the area was very typical of calcareous grassland:—

Common quaking grass	.	*Briza media*
Cocksfoot grass	.	*Dactylus glomerata*
Heath false brome	.	*Brachypodium pinnatum*
Meadow soft grass	.	*Poa pratensis*
False oat grass	.	*Arrhenatherum elatius*
Spotted orchid	.	*Orchis maculata*
Pyramid orchid	.	*Anacamptis pyramidalis*

Bee orchid . . .	*Ophrys apifera*
Germander speedwell .	*Veronica chamaedrys*
Common speedwell . .	*Veronica officinalis*
Field speedwell . .	*Veronica arvensis*
Thyme-leaved speedwell .	*Veronica serpyllifolia*
Yarrow	*Achillea millifolium*
Common daisy . .	*Bellis perennis*
Mouse-ear hawkweed .	*Hieracium pilosella*
Rough Hawksbeard .	*Crepis perennis*
Marsh Thistle . .	*Carduus palustris*
Ox-eye daisy . . .	*Chrysanthemum leucanthemum*
Ploughman's spikenard .	*Inula conyza*
Goat's beard . . .	*Tragopogon pratensis*
Ragwort . . .	*Senecio jacobaea*
Lesser knapweed . .	*Centauria nigra*
Greater Scabious . .	*Knautia arvensis*
Milkwort . . .	*Polygala vulgaris*
Rockrose . . .	*Helianthemum chamaecistus*
Yellow-wort . . .	*Blackstonia perfoliata*
Centaury . . .	*Centaurium minus*
Creeping cinquefoil . .	*Potentilla reptans*
Salad burnet . . .	*Poterium sanguisorba*
Wild strawberry . .	*Fragaria vesca*
Agrimony . . .	*Agrimonia eupatoria*
Violet	*Viola riviniana*
Cathartic flax . .	*Linum catharticum*
Bird's foot trefoil . .	*Lotus corniculatus*
Dyers greenweed . .	*Genista tinctoria*
Meadow pea . . .	*Lathyrus pratensis*
Nonsuch . . .	*Medicago lululina*
Hop trefoil . . .	*Trifolium campestre*
Dutch clover . . .	*Trifolium repens*
Red clover . . .	*Trifolium pratense*
Mouse-ear chickweed .	*Cerastium valgatum*
Field madder . .	*Sherardia arvensis*
Yellow bedstraw . .	*Galium verum*
Hairy St. John's-wort .	*Hypericum hirsutum*

Perforate St. John's-wort			*Hypericum perforatum*
Scarlet pimpernel	.	.	*Anagallis arvensis*
Primrose	.	.	*Primula vulgaris*
Forget-me-not	.	.	*Myosotis sp.*
Thyme	.	.	*Thymus serpyllum*
Calamint	.	.	*Calamintha ascendens*
Selfheal	.	.	*Prunella vulgaris*
Broad-leaved plantain	.		*Plantago media*

These plants, however, were not the only types present, and
there was plenty of evidence that true woodland species had
already become established in a number of places. The most
obvious of these were the shrubs. These were scattered over
the whole area, but were most numerous near to the wood.
They varied in size from tiny seedlings to large bushes. Hawthorn, bramble and dogrose were the most common species,
but privet, wayfaring tree and hazel were also present. It was
significant that the most common, oldest and therefore first
established shrubs had some protection against grazing animals.
Thus hawthorn had its stem spines, and bramble and rose their
prickles. It was logical to suppose that the more delicate
herbaceous woodland plants if they were to become established
in pasture would be able to do so best where there was shade
and protection. This was found to be very obviously the case
when search was made in the vicinity of the shrubs. In fact
nearly all the woodland herbs were found either under or
nearby some well-established shrub. This provided protection
from excessive loss of water through transpiration, and to
some extent from grazing animals. In these places we found
tway-blade orchid (*Listera ovata*), foetid iris (*Iris foetidissima*),
bugle (*Ajuga reptans*), wood spurge (*Euphorbia amygdaloides*),
figwort (*Scrophularia nodosa*), burdock (*Arctium minus*), and
primroses (*Primula vulgaris*). In addition several climbers
were already present making use of the support afforded by
the shrubs. Ivy (*Hedera helix*) was found commonly under
the bushes in the deeper shade, while clematis formed an
intricate mass over the brambles. A few plants of black

bryony (*Tamus communis*) twisted their way to the light and showed above the hawthorns. A little madder (*Rubia peregrina*) was also found.

A careful search was made for young trees becoming established and a number of oaks in the seedling and sapling stages were discovered. One or two maples were also present. The majority of these young trees were difficult to find as they were in the vicinity of the shrubs. Some in fact were beginning to push their way through the bushes, but a few were right out in the open grassland, a fact that bore witness to the lack of grazing by cattle.

When the other area on the east side of the wood was studied the difference was most marked. Here the grazing had been heavy. Bushes of hawthorn, bramble and dogrose were present, but these were the only shrubs found. It was also noticed that they were more isolated. The herbaceous layer contained far fewer species. The grasses were much shorter, and the other types were largely limited to those species which formed rosettes of leaves near to the ground such as plantains, common daisy, salad burnet, cowslip, and mouse-ear hawkweed. This habit appears to have considerable survival value in relation to grazing, especially by cattle. After careful search for some time, two or three tree saplings were discovered; these were in dense bushes, and were oaks.

From these observations it seemed logical to deduce that the first stage in succession from pasture to woodland had been the establishment of shrubs with thorns or prickles which could survive the depredations of grazing animals. These bushes provided the necessary shade for some of the hardier woodland herbs so that they could compete successfully with the grassland species which suffered a corresponding disadvantage. Later still tree seedlings became established especially under the protection of the shrubs. It is probable that these saplings will eventually push their way above the shrub layer, and cast further shade which would kill off more of the pasture types and allow the more delicate woodland species to get a footing. It seemed as if this phase would not be long in coming as far as the south-west area was concerned, but that in the eastern pasture the heavy grazing was sufficient to keep the conditions fairly stable. It was realized that only long-term experimental methods could establish with certainty the exact course of the succession, but the observations on the composition of the present flora in the two areas were sufficient to give a useful indication of the probable stages that had occurred up to the present time.

CONCLUSIONS

In the foregoing pages we have tried to give a broad picture of a woodland community   The emphasis has been on principle rather than detail, because it is so easy when working on a complex community to lose sight of the big picture in a welter of apparently unrelated details.   The ecologist needs both a vision of the wholeness of life as well as appreciation of the importance of detail ; the two are complementary.   He needs a general, though inevitably this must be a rather vague picture of the whole jig-saw puzzle, in order to appreciate the position and relationships of the few species he is able to study in detail.

In a booklet of this type and scope it was not possible to introduce more detail than was necessary to bring out the main points, but it is hoped that it will suggest more detailed lines of investigation.   The study of many of the microhabitats has not been alluded to in detail although they provide excellent fields for study.   There is also tremendous scope in the method of concentrating on one species of importance in the community, and working out its various relationships both to the other organisms and the complex of environmental factors.

So in conclusion let us attempt to bring together the main principles we have tried to outline and picture the woodland community as a living whole—as a gigantic jig-saw puzzle in three dimensions whose shape is determined by the floral scaffolding.   The relationships between individual pieces may appear at first to be rather rigid, but further study shows that this is usually far from the case.   We find that there is an essential fluidity, which compensates for the changes which are all the time occurring in the community.   We might think of the pieces as being at times amœboid in nature, altering their shape as adaptations to changing conditions.   Sometimes due to rhythmic changes of daily or seasonal occurrence, this whole picture of the community may alter, and much re-shuffling of the parts take place.

We see, too, that there is interdependence between the parts ; although so different in size and importance, all are of significance to the whole, and to varying extents depend on the rest for their existence. There is also a delicate balance of give and take between the different parts—a balance which if upset may lead to the alteration of the whole picture. This, in fact, is always occurring as one species increases and affects the numbers of another, but soon a new equilibrium is produced.

Finally, we have to superimpose on this picture the essentially dynamic nature of woodland, its potential power for expansion and its intricate links with other surrounding communities. What has been said of woodland could be said of these, each is not a watertight parcel, many types move from one community to another, linking them together. So we are led to the conception that all life is really a unity—a magnificent complex of inter-related parts, the full beauty of which is beyond all powers of comprehension.

APPENDIX

THERE is no perfect method of carrying out an ecological survey. Circumstances alter so much from school to school that what is good for one may be impossible for another. However, the following notes based on my own experience may be helpful in providing ideas which the teacher can modify according to his own circumstances.

In most schools, those taking biology in a sixth form are of three grades, those in the first year who have little or no experience of ecological work, those in the second year who have already done a little, and a small group composed of those who are studying for scholarships. I have found it best to start off those in the first year with a general survey of the wood in the pre-vernal aspect, and if possible to make further visits in May, late June, October and December. During this year more stress is laid on the botanical side, although the animals are by no means neglected. During the second year a general revision of the flora is carried out, paying special attention to gaps in previous observations and any special problems that have arisen. The animals are now studied more extensively. The more detailed work and individual projects are left to the scholarship boys and anyone in either year who has sufficient keenness and general knowledge of natural history to do a good deal on his own.

In the suggestions that follow, some things can be done by the whole class, others by individuals or small groups during the few organized surveys, and still others which are particularly suitable for the scholarship boy or the keen naturalist.

The important thing is that all the work can then be integrated so that a general picture emerges which all can appreciate, and there is no reason why the study should not go on for a number of years with different groups, more and more detail being collected. In the latter event the basic first year work has to be repeated each year with the new set.

When carrying out studies in small groups it is well to change over occupations at intervals so that each gets some knowledge of method. This also provides a means of checking results and exposing errors of the more obvious kind.

(1) FIRST VISIT TO SHOW PRE-VERNAL ASPECT

The best time for this varies according to season and locality. In the south if it is an early season the last half of March is good. In the north it may be better to wait until late April.

A general survey is first made by the whole class to familiarize each with the general topography. Duplicated outline maps are most useful ; they are best taken from large-scale Ordnance Survey maps and prepared beforehand. On- this occasion the zonation is noted and any marked variation in the flora. Plants in flower should be identified and the distribution of the dominants noted. Microhabitats can be pointed out so that any observations on animals made during any visit can be related to them. The relative frequencies of the flowering members of the field layer should also be assessed and any pollinating agents noted.

(2) THE VERNAL ASPECT

The first half of May is often the best time in the south for this visit.

All trees and shrubs should be identified and their frequencies estimated. Also, all new plants found in flower should be identified and their frequencies noted. Further observations should be made on pollinating agents. Specimens of all the more common types should be dug up to show their rooting systems and underground storage organs. These should be taken back for further examination in the laboratory.

(3) THE ÆSTIVAL ASPECT

Any time between mid-June and the end of July.

All plants in flower should be listed and new ones identified. Any adaptations to the shade phase should be recorded including leaf mosaic. Pre-vernal types should now be dying and should be noted. Light intensity measurements should be made in the various layers and compared with those taken in the open. Humidity experiments using an atmometer should also be done. Leaf litter should be brought back in a small sack and its fauna examined later in the laboratory. Soil samples should also be taken back for analysis.

(4) AUTUMNAL ASPECT

Any time from late September to the end of October.

Fruit dispersal mechanisms of woodland plants can be studied, and the condition of the plants in the field layer noted. Fungi, mosses and liverworts should be collected and taken back for identification. Another sample of leaf litter should be collected for analysis.

(5) HIEMAL ASPECT
Any time between December and February.

The winter condition of plants can be studied, including the degree of protection given to the winter buds. The winter activities of animals should be noted. Bird counts should be made to show feeding preference habitats. This is a good time to study the under-bark community and to compare it with that found in the summer. More leaf litter should be analysed and soil samples can again be taken for comparison.

Much more work can be done on animals during the year if time permits.

The following can best be done by individuals over a longer period of time :

(1) The general study of a single species of plant or animal from every possible aspect, e.g. life history, feeding habits distribution, enemies, numbers, etc.

(2) A study of the methods of vegetative reproduction of woodland plants.

(3) A study of the rooting systems and effective root depths of typical members of the field layer.

(4) To test the effectiveness of pollination methods by means of flower counts, seed counts and the viability of the seeds. Also a comparison between those of the same species growing in deep shade and in more open parts.

(5) To illustrate succession by means of a permanent quadrat set up on areas which have been coppiced or felled.

(6) To determine the change in flora resulting from variation in water content of the soil by using a line transect and analysing the soil at intervals down the transect.

(7) Identification of the fauna obtained by beating the dominant tree, and dividing the animals up according to feeding habits. This should be done at different seasons and the species and numbers compared.

(8) General study of all woodland birds seen during the year in terms of food, nesting habits, territory, migration, etc.

(9) Further work on the variation in the fauna of leaf litter both in numbers and species in square metre samples taken at regular times from the same area.

(10) To determine the variation in number of springtails and mites in soil according to depth using a Berlese funnel.

(11) A study of the following microhabitats :
Under bark.

> Under logs.
> In the moss and lichens of tree trunks (using a Berlese funnel).
> In carrion. This is best done by baiting (with suitable material) jam-jars sunk in the ground.
> Tree holes.

(12) Dung and pellet analysis whenever found, e.g. of fox, badger, owls.

(13) To find the effect of (a) rabbits, (b) voles and mice on the vegetation of the herb layer using different meshed wire netting sunk into the ground.

(14) To estimate the species of small rodents found in the wood by live-trapping.

(15) Map out any badger sets and paths. Watch sets at dusk and note badger behaviour. See if sets are occupied all the year round, and if not, determine where they go, when and why. Do counts regularly through the year and note when major changes occur. Note when fresh bedding is brought into the sets.

(16) Make a general study of camouflage in woodland animals.

(17) Make an estimation of the earthworm population of woodland soil by the potassium permanganate method. Identify the species if possible.

(18) Determine the effect of putting up nest boxes on the number of nesting birds such as tits in the wood.

BIBLIOGRAPHY

THE following is a small selection from the vast numbers of books and papers of interest to ecologists. They are selected as being particularly valuable for further reading on various aspects of woodland ecology mentioned in this booklet.

GENERAL WORKS

BRADE-BIRKS, S. G. (1944). *Good Soil.* English Universities Press.

BROOKES, B. C., and DICK, W. F. L. (1951). *An Introduction to Statistical Method.* Heinemann.

CHRYSTAL, R. N. (1937). *Insects of the British Woodlands.* Warne.

CLARKE, G. R. *The Study of Soil in the Field.* Oxford University Press.

COTT, H. B. (1940). *Adaptive Coloration in Animals.* Methuen.

DOWDESWELL, W. H. (1952). *Animal Ecology.* Methuen.

ELTON, C. (1926). *Animal Ecology.* Sidgwick & Jackson.

ELTON, C. (1933). *The Ecology of Animals.* Methuen.

HOWARD, H. E. (1948). *Territory in Bird Life.* Collins.

IMMS, A. D. (1947). *Insect Natural History.* Collins.

MATTHEWS, L. H. (1952). *British Mammals.* Collins.

MCLEAN, R. C., and COOK, W. R. I. (1943). *Practical Field Ecology.* Allen & Unwin.

NEAL, E. (1948). *The Badger.* Collins.

TANSLEY, A. G. (1939). *The British Islands and their Vegetation.* Cambridge.

TANSLEY, A. G. (1946). *Introduction to Plant Ecology.* Allen & Unwin.

TURRILL, W. B. (1948). *British Plant Life.* Collins.

PAPERS

ADAMSON, R. S. (1925). *The Woodlands of Ditcham Park, Hants.* J. Ecol., 13.

BAKER, H., and CLAPHAM, A. R. (1939). *Seasonal Variation in the Acidity of some Woodland Soils.* J. Ecol., 27.

COLQUHOUN, M. K., and MORLEY, A. (1943). *Vertical Zonation in Woodland Bird Communities.* J. Anim. Ecol., 12, *pages 75–81.*

COLQUHOUN, M. K. (1940). *The Density of Woodland Birds Determined by the Sample Count Method.* J. Anim. Ecol., 9, *pages 53–67.*

ELTON, C. (1935). *A Reconnaissance of Woodland Bird Communities in England and Wales.* J. Anim. Ecol., 4, *pages* 127–36.

GARNETT, T. R. (1950). *Bird Watching to some Purpose.* Biology, 15, No. 4, *pages* 187–92.

LACK, D., and VENABLES, L. S. V. (1939). *The Habitat Distributions of British Woodland Birds.* J. Anim. Ecol., 8, *pages* 39–71.

MUCKERGI, S. K. (1936). *Contributions to the Autecology of Mercurialis perennis, L.* J. Ecol., 24.

SALISBURY, E. J. (1921). *Stratification of H-ion Concentration of the Soil in Relation to Leaching and Plant Succession with Special Reference to Woodlands.* J. Ecol., 9.

SALISBURY, E. J. (1925). *The Vegetation of the Forest of Wyre.* J. Ecol., 13.

SUMMERHAYES, V. S. (1941). *The Effect of Voles on Vegetation.* J. Ecol., 29, *pages* 14–48.

WATTS, A. S. (1919). *On the Cause of Failure of Natural Regeneration in British Oakwoods.* J. Ecol., 7.

BOOKS SELECTED TO AID IDENTIFICATION

Animals

Crustacea

Woodlice   EDNEY, E. B. (1953). *The Woodlice of Great Britain and Ireland.* Proc. Linn. Soc. Keys to genera and species.

Insecta

Orthoptera   BURR, M. (1936). *British Grasshoppers and their Allies.* Phillip Allan. Keys to adults. Plates.

     LUCAS, W. J. (1920). *Monograph of the British Orthoptera.* Ray Society.

Odonata   LONGFIELD, C. (1937). *The Dragonflies of the British Isles.* Warne. Keys to adults. Coloured plates. Very useful.

Hemiptera   SAUNDERS, E. (1892). *The Hemiptera Heteroptera of the British Isles.* Reeve. An old book long out of print, but with excellent plates. 52 species have since been added and much of the nomenclature is out of date.

     EDWARDS, J. (1896). *The Hemiptera Homoptera of the British Isles.* Reeve. Companion volume to " Saunders."

Lepidoptera   SOUTH, R. (1906). *Butterflies of the British Isles.* Warne. Coloured plates.

SOUTH, R. (1939). *Moths of the British Isles.* Warne. Coloured plates of the majority of British moths except for the microlepidoptera.

FROWHAWK, F. W. (1934). *The Complete Book of British Butterflies.* Ward, Lock. Coloured plates of all stages.

STOKOE, W. J., and STOVIN, G. H. T. (1944). *The Caterpillars of the British Butterflies.* Warne. Coloured plates.

STOKOE, W. J. (1949). *The Caterpillars of the British Moths.* Coloured plates.

MEYRICK, E. (1927). *Revised Handbook of the British Lepidoptera.* Watkins and Doncaster. Includes the Microlepidoptera. Keys.

Coleoptera   FOWLER, W. E. (1887–91). *Coleoptera of the British. Isles.* Reeve. A rare book long out of print with excellent coloured plates of most of the genera. Keys to species. Out of date, but still very uesful.

JOY, N. H. (1932). *Practical Handbook of British Beetles.* Witherby. Line illustrations. Keys to species.

Hymenoptera   STEP, E. (1932). *Bees, wasps, ants, and allied insects of the British Isles.* Warne. Coloured plates. Only of slight use for identification.

DONISTHORPE, H. (1927). *British Ants.* Plates and keys.

Diptera   MARSHALL, J. F. (1938). *The British Mosquitoes.* British Museum. Keys and coloured plates.

COLYER, C. N., and HAMMOND, C. O. (1951). *Flies of the British Isles.* Warne. Excellent coloured plates, but keys stop at families.

Arachnida   TODD, V. (1948). *Key to the determination of the British Harvestmen.* Ent. Mon. Mag. 84, pp. 109–113.

LOCKET and MILLIDGE (1951). *British Spiders.* Excellent for identification, but difficult to use without good working knowledge of the group.

Mollusca   STEP, E. (1937). *Shell Life.* Warne. Coloured plates. Good for the larger species.

ELLIS, A. E. (1926). *British Snails.* Keys to genera.

QUICK, H. E. (1949). *Slugs.* Synopses Brit. Fauna, No. 8. Linn. Soc. London. Keys to genera. Text figures.

Reptilla and SMITH, M. A. (1951). *British Reptiles and Amphibians.*
Amphibia   Collins. Excellent for identification and general
                   information. Coloured plates.
Aves   COWARD, T. A. (1919–1926). *The Birds of the British
                   Isles and their Eggs.* Warne. Coloured plates.
                   Very useful.
                WITHERBY, JORDAIN, TICEHURST, and TUCKER. *The
                   Handbook of the British Birds.* Witherby. The
                   standard work on the group. Coloured plates of all
                   species.
                PETERSON, MOUNTFORD and HOLLOM. (1954). *Field
                   Guide io the Birds of Britain and Europe.* Collins.
                   Excellent for identification in the field and com-
                   paratively easy to use.
Mammalia   MORRISON-SCOTT, T. C. S. (1952). *A List of British
                   Mammals.* British Museum. Keys and illustra-
                   tions. Very useful.
                MATTHEWS, L. H. (1952). *British Mammals.* Collins.
                   Coloured plates. Excellent for general information.

Plants

Fungi   RAMSBOTTOM, J. (1951). *Handbook of the Larger
                   British Fungi.* British Museum. Very useful for
                   those with some knowledge of the group. Keys.
                WAKEFIELD AND DENNIS, *Common British Fungi.*
                   Gawthorn. Good coloured plates. Keys.
Lichens   SMITH, A. L. (1921). *Handbook of the British Lichens.*
                   British Museum. Difficult to use without a good
                   knowledge of the group.
Mosses   WATSON, H. (1947). *Woodland mosses.* Forestry
                   Commission booklet. Useful illustrations.
                DIXON, H. N. (1924). *Students Handbook of British
                   Mosses.* Sumfield. Rather out of date, but com-
                   prehensive.
                WATSON, E. V. (1955). *British Mosses and Liverworts.*
                   Cambridge University Press. Very useful.
Liverworts   MACVICAR, S. M. (1926). *Students Handbook of British
                   Hepatics.* Sumfield. Rather out of date, but very
                   useful. Keys to genera and species.
                WATSON, E. V. (1955). *British Mosses and Liverworts.*
Ferns   STEP, E. *Wayside and Woodland Ferns.* Warne.
                   Coloured plates.

Angiosperms and Gymnosperms	CLAPHAM, TUTIN and WARBURG (1952). *Flora of the British Isles.* Cambridge University Press. Comprehensive up-to date flora.

BENTHAM and HOOKER (1947). *Handbook of the British Flora.* Reeve. Rather out-of-date, but still very useful.

FITCH, W. H. and SMITH, W. G. (1946). *Illustrations of the British Flora.* Very useful. Line drawings of all common species.

BUTCHER, R. W. and STRUDWICK, F. E. (1946). *Further Illustrations of the British Flora.* Reeve. Very useful.

MATKINS, F. K. (1936). *Identification of Trees and Shrubs.* Dent. Well illustrated.

ROSS-CRAIG, S. *Drawings of British Plants.* Parts 1–8 published so far. Bell. Excellent. Drawings only.

HUBBARD, C. E. (1954). *Grasses.* Penguin Books. Very useful.

INDEX

Heavy numerals indicate an illustration or table